Planting the
Natural Garden

For Anja

Planting the
Natural Garden

Piet Oudolf Henk Gerritsen

TIMBER PRESS
Portland • Cambridge

Photo cover:
Pensthorpe Waterfowl Park, Fakenham, Norfolk

Published in the English language in 2003 by
Timber Press, Inc.
The Haseltine Building
133 S.W. Second Avenue, Suite 450
Portland, Oregon
97204-3527, U.S.A.

Timber Press
2 Station Road
Swavesey
Cambridge CB4 5QJ
U.K.

ISBN 0-88192-606-X

Catalog records for this book are available from the
Library of Congress and the British Library.

Text: Henk Gerritsen and Piet Oudolf
Photography: Anton Schlepers, Piet Oudolf and Henk Gerritsen
Translation: Susanne Tonkens-Hart
Graphic design: Varwig Design, Erik de Bruin, Hengelo (NL)
Printed in Belgium: Proost NV, Turnhout

Contents

Introduction   6

Plant descriptions

Perennials   10

Ornamental Grasses   76

Uses   84

Blazing   88

Lush   92

Airy   96

Tranquillity   100

Exuberant   104

Silvery   108

Grassy   112

Gloomy?   116

Autumn   120

Wonderful   124

Good Neighbors   128

Planting Plans   130

Exceptional Properties of Plants   132

Plants per Square Meter   136

Literature List   138

Photographic Acknowledgments   139

Nurseries and Gardens   139

Index   140

Explanation of the symbols

☼ Sun
(at least 7 hours of sun a day in summer)

◑ Semi-shade
(filtered sunlight or 3-5 hours of sun)

● Shade
(less than 3 hours of sun in summer)

↕ Height (in cm)

❀ Flowering time (1 = January; 2 = February; etc.)

Introduction

In the autumn of 1982, when the first catalog from de Koesterd, the nursery of Piet and Anja Oudolf and Romke van der Kaa, dropped through the letterbox, I could never have imagined that it would one day lead to a book. On the contrary, I read the catalog with mounting amazement for I knew hardly any of the plants. And although the descriptions seemed to be about all kinds of interesting plants for wild garden enthusiasts, I strongly doubted the plants' winter hardiness and use in the garden. I phoned the nursery and said, in a friendly fashion, "Thanks for the catalog, very nice," but added, in a slightly less friendly manner, "I'll drop 'round in the spring and see which plants have survived the winter."

Since then I have closely followed the ups and downs of de Kesterd. Romke van der Kaa left in 1985 to set up his own nursery at Ellecom in eastern Netherlands, which he has since given up, and the Oudolfs have succeeded, by trial and error, in building up a completely new assortment of garden plants that excel in their suitability for contemporary gardens: fully hardy, strong, easy to grow, and so forth. The "completely new" is especially applicable to the appearance of the plants: not only do they look wilder and flower in subtler shades than was the case with the "old" assortment, but also much more attention has been paid to such aspects as shape, texture, and the appearance of the plants after flowering (seed heads, autumn colors, and the winter silhouette) than was the case in the past.

The wild garden

Since the end of the sixties there has been a widespread awareness of the rapid disappearance of our wild flowers. I remember cycling around Utrecht at the beginning of the sixties and seeing ditches filled with marsh lousewort (*Pedicularis palustris*) and fields overgrown with sun spurge (*Euphorbia helioscopia*) and scarlet pimpernel (*Anagallis arvensis*). The water meadows of the river Lek were covered with ox-eye daisies (*Leucanthemum vulgare*), yellow rattle (*Rhinanthus angustifolius*), and rough hawk's beard (*Crepis biennis*); ten years later all had disappeared. In the meantime, my biology teacher was telling us lyrical tales about the Gagel Polder near Utrecht in pre-war days: millions of orchids as far as the eye could see, a profusion of purple everywhere. And when you read descriptions of the countryside around 1900, you don't wonder why there was little interest in wild plants for the garden—there were still so many in the outside world.

At the time the last surviving plants had almost disappeared, gardening with indigenous plants was gaining momentum as a last resort for conserving our wild flowers. In the seventies, the very extreme ideas of the art teacher from Heerenveen (in northern Netherlands), Louis de Roy, who rejected almost all forms of garden maintenance, had their short-lived heyday. It soon became obvious that waxing lyrical about plants like stinging nettles and couch grass had

more to do with "Minimal Art" than with gardening. Of course stinging nettles are wonderful. On closer consideration, all plants are of wonderful design, but because stinging nettles belong to a select group of plants that are profiting from the loss of the wild flora, we do not really need to cherish them in the garden as well.

Gardening with indigenous plants in private gardens turned out, in practice, to be disappointing. Most species have such small flowers that they have to be planted in large groups to have any effect and, in general, the gardens were too small. All kinds of species that look beautiful growing amid the grass in a poor meadow were not half as attractive in the garden. One example is the field scabious (*Knautia arvensis*): in the garden the 80-cm-high stalks collapse in a tangled mess onto the ground—dreadful! Most wild plants need poor soil and, in general, garden soil is too fertile. In short, the experiment with indigenous plants ended for many gardeners in a flop. But the desire for more nature in the garden remained because the numbers of wild flowers were still diminishing. In fact, ordinary meadow plants like lady's smock, buttercup, and sorrel were seen less frequently. This situation created, as it were, a gap in the market. The old-established assortment of garden plants was considered by many to have been overcultivated and too unnatural. The indigenous plants turned out to be, with a few exceptions, unsuitable for gardens, so nursery owners went in search of plants that could fill the gap: plants with the same reliable qualities as the well-known, established ornamental plants but with a wilder, more natural appearance.

The plants

This search has been carried out systematically by Piet and Anja Oudolf. Seeds of wild plants were ordered from Europe, Korea, Japan, China, Kashmir, and North America, with the intention of trying them out for their usefulness in the garden.

Throughout Europe, and later the United States, the Oudolfs searched well-known and lesser-known nurseries for rarities that could be added to the new assortment. Strangely enough, they found quite a few species that had been grown a hundred years previously, such as numerous varieties of

Sanguisorba and *Thalictrum*, but subsequently pushed aside as being uninteresting (too wild). Now that they have been rediscovered, these plants can be safely considered the most popular of the new assortment: they are strong and very hardy, grow on almost any type of soil, have very interesting leaf shapes and ways of growing, and look extremely wild.

At the same time, the Oudolfs were trying to find improved varieties. For example, from whorled clary (*Salvia verticillata)*, a grubby-looking plant with lavender-blue florets growing in whorls around the stems, they found the cultivar 'Purple Rain', the florets of which are borne on purple-stained stems. This cultivar has more effect than the original species, without losing its wild appearance. The Oudolfs also searched within the established assortment for forms that met with changing tastes. For example, *Monarda* 'Fishes' is a cultivar of the bergamot plant with subtle, shell pink lipped flowers around a gray-green center. In the past, such a culti-

var would have been cast aside as not being spectacular enough, but shortly after its introduction at de Koesterd there was a tremendous run on it. You cannot imagine a present-day garden without the age-old, almost forgotten masterwort *(Astrantia major)* thanks to the deep, dark red 'Claret' and the antique-rose-colored 'Roma' from the Oudolf nursery. The same applies, and to a far greater extent, to ornamental grasses that until recently, after Karl Foerster had called our attention to them in the fifties, could only be admired in gardens and parks that had been laid out by professional designers, and then only occasionally.

The uses

In the Priona gardens, which I laid out at Schuinesloot in northeastern Netherlands in 1978 with photographer Anton Schlepers, who died in 1993, I have increasingly been using this new assortment. Because I attempt to keep the gardens as natural and wild as possible, these plants have fitted in perfectly. When designing gardens for others, these plants have also become indispensable. After seeing the Priona gardens, clients regularly request that I design something similar for them. However, it is generally a lack of know-how and time that prevents them from learning to balance on the brink of total wilderness, just as I do, without their gardens deteriorating into utter chaos. The assortment that the Oudolf nursery has developed since the eighties—plants that look wild but do not behave in a wild manner—is pre-eminently suitable for creating the natural aspect in the garden that the clients desire, and which they do not need to be experts in order to maintain.

The place to see what can be achieved with the new assortment is naturally the ever-changing garden around Piet and Anja's nursery at Hummelo in the eastern province of Gelderland. That many people, in the meantime, have been convinced by what can be seen there becomes apparent when considering the many prestigious garden designs that Piet Oudolf has realized at home and abroad in recent years: the Drömparken in Enköping, Sweden; the planting outside the head office of the ABN-AMRO Bank in Amsterdam; two immense borders in the gardens of the Royal Horticultural Society in Wisley, near London; the Millennium Garden in Chicago (together with Kathryn Gustafson); and The Battery at the southernmost tip of Manhattan.

The book

By the end of the eighties the plant assortment developed by Anja and Piet Oudolf had created a lot of excitement among Dutch garden lovers, and there was a great demand for a book describing the assortment. The honor of writing this book fell to me, as one of the instigators, along with Piet and Anja Oudolf, Rob Leopold, Coen Jansen, and others, of what later became known as "The Dutch Wave." Anton Schlepers was asked to take photographs for the book. On countless occasions Anton visited the Oudolf garden to photograph plants in the scorching summer of 1989, an almost inhuman task when you realize that on most days the temperature rose to above 30 degrees Celsius. The result of his work is all the more astonishing.

Later, in the winter of 1989–1990, I started writing the book. With freezing feet despite an electric heater, and using a dilapidated, borrowed word processor, I sat in the back of my farmhouse in Schuinesloot and wrote. Titled *Droomplanten* ("Dream Plants"), the book was launched at de Koesterd in the autumn of 1990. A similarly successful sequel appeared in 1999 as *Meer Droomplanten* ("More Dream Plants") and was published in English as *Dream Plants for the Natural Garden*. Although the Dutch title is not very inspiring, it actually covers the contents: more than twice as many plants are described in the sequel than in the original. The new, completely revised third edition which you hold in your hands was compiled when the original book, which had never been translated into English, went out of print.

Demand for that book is still great, and with so much interest in it in both the United Kingdom and the United States, it was decided to publish the book again, with the necessary changes to bring the information up-to-date. Some of the plant species that proved during the past thirteen years to be less reliable than we first presumed have been scrapped, and a number of new species and cultivars have been added. In the section on plant uses, the chapters "Airy" and "Sturdy" have been merged in this edition, and a new chapter titled "Gloomy?" describes plants as they appear in late autumn and during the winter. The lists of plant combinations in the chapters "Wonderful" and "Good Neighbors", as well as the number of suggested species in the chapter "Plants per Square Meter", have been critically studied since the original book was published and, where necessary, adapted to reflect our experience in the intervening years. Moreover, it was possible to add a large number of photographs to this edition, so that the book has become even more attractive than it was.

Henk Gerritsen

Perennials

Achillea, Asteraceae, _yarrow_

An important genus for the garden, especially because of the unusual inflorescence, a flat, pancakelike flower head, whose form is indispensable among the numerous spike- and cluster-shaped inflorescences in the garden.

Achillea hybrids

☼　↕ 60-120　✼ 6-9

Gardeners may be familiar with the pink forms of the extremely common, white-flowering milfoil (_A. millefolium_), which sometimes crop up spontaneously. By crossing them with yellow-flowering species from southern Europe, hybrids in all the colors of the rainbow have originated, so that the "pancake" form can be used in almost every imaginable color combination. Unfortunately, the hybrids are often unreliable plants that disappear after a few years. The only solution is to dig up and rejuvenate the plants every two years.

'Credo'
A tall-growing (100 cm) cultivar with sulfur-yellow flowers.

'Hella Glashoff'
An attractive, pale yellow cultivar that does not grow very tall.

'Lilac Beauty'
Similar to the pink species that occurs in the wild, with small pale lilac flower heads. Extremely free-flowering.

'Schwefelblüte'
A sulfur-yellow cultivar that does not grow very tall.

'Summerwine'
Flowers wine red, color not fading as in the other hybrids, but turning deep purple.

'Walther Funcke'
A coarse, gray-leaved plant that only reaches about 70 cm. Its flowers are bright red with yellow centers.

'Wesersandstein'
Magenta-pink flowers fade to pale yellow, so that the plant bears two different colors at the same time. Spectacular.

Aconitum, Ranunculaceae, _monkshood_

Free-flowering plants that belong to the fascinating buttercup family, which includes buttercup, anemone, delphinium, old man's beard, hellebore, rue, and columbine, to mention a few. Yet the buttercup family, which shows so much variety, is considered one of the oldest and, therefore, most primitive plant families. All the monkshood species have attractive, often glossy, more or less palmate foliage and curiously shaped flowers that, with a little imagination, resemble a monk's hood. The flowers are pollinated only by bumblebees.

A. carmichaelii var. _wilsonii_

☼　◐　↕ 180　✼ 9-10

One of the first perennials to appear in spring, but producing flowers almost always at the end of the season. Beautiful purple-blue flowers, exceptional in autumn. A strong plant that never flops over.

A. episcopale

☼　◐　↕ 250　✼ 8-10

A plant with lilac-colored flowers and twining stems, suitable for climbing in small shrubs or (sturdy) tall perennials. Unreliable, but when it does take, on fertile, moisture-retentive soil, everyone exclaims, "What on earth is that?"

A. lamarckii

☼　◐　↕ 90　✼ 7-8

A relatively strong form of the yellow monkshood (_A. lycoctonum s.l._), with tall, sulfur-yellow flowers. Relatively, because all the yellow-flowering species collapse easily. Instead of tying them up (ugly), plant them between sturdy perennials or small shrubs, against which they can lean.

A. napellus

This is the ordinary purple-blue common or garden monkshood that everyone knows. It is included in this book because of the beautiful white (**'Grandiflorum Album'**), pink (**'Pink Sensation'**), and pale blue (**'Stainless Steel'**) varieties that are now available.

A. septentrionale 'Ivorine'

☼　◐　↕ 50　✼ 5-6

One of the few garden plants to hail from Scandinavia, where it flowers in summer, as befits a monkshood. In the Netherlands, where spring arrives far earlier, _A. septentrionale_ flowers "by mistake" in May and June. The plant remains relatively low and has fresh green, glossy foliage and ivory-colored flowers.

Actaea, Ranunculaceae
herb Christopher, baneberry

Indispensable plants for shady spots. Foliage is composite pinnate or bipinnate, and flowers are small white or yellowish on short (herb Christopher) or elongated (baneberry) spikes. In the wild, these plants grow in damp woods or ravines, where the sun seldom shines. In gardens they can tolerate a good deal of sun, provided the soil does not dry out. Should that occur, the plants shrivel up before your eyes. The ornamental value of herb Christopher lies in its striking summer berries, while that of baneberry, better known under the old scientific name _Cimicifuga_, resides in the whole habit and the eye-catching inflorescence in late summer. For simplicity's sake, we shall first discuss herb Christopher, then baneberry.

herb Christopher

A. pachypoda

◐　●　↕ 90　✼ 5-6

Bears white berries on thick, dark red stems.

A. rubra

◐　●　↕ 40　✼ 5-6

Bears shiny, red berries on red stems. _Actaea rubra_ f. _neglecta_ grows much taller (80 cm) and has white berries. Another form, which bears translucent orange-red berries, is occasionally available as _A. rubra_ **'Neglecta'**.

A. spicata

◐　●　↕ 50　✼ 5-6

Bears black berries.

baneberry

A. cordifolia

◐　●　↕ 140　✼ 8-9

Has palmate foliage, not heart shaped as the scientific name promises, and attractive yellowish-green flower spikes.

A. heracleifolia

The sturdy flower stems, which are branched at the top, bear several upward-pointing, arching flower spikes towards the end of the year.

A. japonica

☽ ● ↕ 100 ✿ 8-9

The shortest baneberry, with metallic-colored, shiny foliage and short, candlelike flower spikes.

A. mairei

☽ ● ↕ 140 ✿ 9-10

Spikes slightly drooping. The yellowish flowers have a touch of orange on the petals. Most elegant.

A. simplex var. matsumurae 'White Pearl'

☽ ● ↕ 120 ✿ 10

One of the last baneberries to flower. Compact, luminous-white, half-pendent spikes.

A. simplex var. simplex 'Atropurpurea'

☽ ↕ 200 ✿ 9-10

A giant plant with purple-red foliage and elongated flower "candles." The white flowers have purple-red calyces and flower stems. This very strong plant never collapses. The red of the foliage intensifies in full sunlight. Watch that the soil does not dry out.
simplex var. *simplex* '**James Compton**'
Slightly shorter (180 cm) than 'Atropurpurea', with dark foliage and harmoniously placed flower stems.
simplex var. *simplex* '**Prichard's Giant**'
An immense giant (220 cm) with dull green foliage. Way above the leaves, the flower spikes appear to be floating in the wind.
simplex var. *simplex* '**Scimitar**'
Resembles 'Prichard's Giant' but is slightly shorter (200 cm). Has graceful, arched flower spikes.

Adelocaryum see Lindelofia

Agastache, Lamiaceae, *giant hyssop*

Wonderful garden plants; everything is "just right" about them. Extremely strong stems—the plants cannot collapse, even if you should want them to—with foliage resembling that of the stinging nettle (*Urtica dioica*). The foliage, however, differs in three important ways: it does not sting, it is covered in a purple haze (especially the young leaves), and it has a delicious smell of aniseed (*Pimpinella anisum*). The plants produce flowers over a long period and have tall gray spikes from which small flowers peep. The flowers are frequented by bees and butterflies. The winter silhouette is also beauti-

ful. Blue tits and bullfinches peck at the seeds throughout the winter, giving the gardener a reason to not cut down the plants. Another reason is that the plants are often short-lived, so they should be given an opportunity to self-seed.

A. nepetoides

☼ ↕ 160 ✿ 7-9

A tall, slender species with green spikes. An "exclamation mark" in the garden throughout the winter.

A. rugosa

☼ ↕ 80 ✿ 7-9

A tall species from Korea. The long, green spikes are full of small purple flowers. '**Alabaster**' has white flowers. '**Blue Fortune**' has shiny foliage, dark spikes, and flowers that tend towards blue; it is sterile, so not self-seeding, but does last longer.

Alcea, Malvaceae, *hollyhock*

A description of the hollyhock would seem unnecessary: everyone recognizes the tall, unbranched flower stems around which numerous, five-petaled, regularly formed flowers are grouped. The leaves are broad and lobed. Hollyhocks have a short life: two or three years, a fourth or fifth at a stretch, but then it is over. They tend to seed better between stones and in gravel, less frequently in ordinary garden soil. The species described should not really bear the name; they are probably original crossbreedings. Hollyhocks have been grown since time immemorial, so that no one knows to which "true" species the cultivars belong.

A. ficifolia

☼ ↕ 150 ✿ 7-9

Closely related to or identical to *A. rugosa*, with slightly deeper indented leaves and pale yellow flowers.

A. rosea 'Nigra'

☼ ↕ 150 ✿ 7-9

The "black" hollyhock bears shiny, deep dark red flowers.

Alchemilla, Rosaceae, *lady's mantle*

Low-growing plants with distinctive broad, grayish-green pleated leaves and greenish-yellow sprays of flowers. The flowers never pro-

duce fertile pollen; they reproduce apomictically (that is, asexually). This has resulted in hundreds of species being described, which are impossible for the average person to tell apart: each slightly different parent plant brings forth offspring that all show the same variance. All the various "species" can be placed into one of two groups: *A. vulgaris,* to which, among others, the familiar *A. mollis* belongs, and *A. alpina*. From both groups one example.

A. conjuncta

☀ ↕ 20 ✿ 5-6

Leaves broad, dark green, covered in silky hairs on the underside and around the edges. The small flowers are silvery green. Good ground cover for dry spots.

A. erythropoda

☼ ☽ ↕ 20 ✿ 5-6

A miniature example of the more familiar lady's mantle but slightly greener in all aspects. Ideal for filling up gaps.

Althaea, Malvaceae, *mallow*

A. 'Parkallee'

☼ ↕ 180 ✿ 7-8

An old, long-forgotten cultivar that popped up in Germany after the fall of the Berlin wall. Somewhat like a hollyhock, with gray downy, triangular leaves and cream-colored semidouble flowers with a peach-colored center. How can such a beautiful plant have been forgotten?

Amsonia, Apocynaceae

A long-lived plant with narrow, hairless leaves and racemes of pale blue starlike flowers, in which one can easily recognize affinity with the lesser periwinkle (*Vinca minor*). All the species except one are from North America.

A. hubrichtii

☼ ☽ ↕ 70 ✿ 6-7

The decorative value of this plant is mainly due to the needle-shaped leaves, which turn a wonderful shade of yellow and orange in autumn. The small racemes of pale blue flowers in early summer are an added attraction.

Above
Achillea 'Hella Glashoff'

Far left
Aconitum napellus
'Pink Sensation'

Left
Alcea rosea 'Nigra'

Above right
Actaea simplex
'Scimitar'

Right
Alchemilla erythropoda

A. orientalis

☀ ↕ 40 ✿ 6-8

Syn. *Rhazya orientalis*. A native of Thrace to the northwest of Turkey, this plant shows a slightly rampant growth but never becomes a nuisance. During a warm summer and in a sunny spot, it flowers profusely over a long period, producing tiny steel-blue stars that emerge from dark blue buds. After a shower of rain, which it obviously does not like, the plant collapses into a mess but always straightens up again.

A. tabernaemontana var. *salicifolia*

☀ ◑ ↕ 70 ✿ 6-7

A strong, slow-growing but extremely long-lasting and easy plant, which eventually forms solid clumps. Appears in spring, when purple stems push up through the soil and later bear striking racemes of flowers. Beautiful autumn coloring is also part of the bargain. In other words, this is an excellent garden plant.

Anemone, Ranunculaceae, anenome

Once again a fascinating genus from the buttercup family. Through the ages many species have been grown. Two of them are *A. coronaria*, the florist's anenome, and the incomparable herald of spring, *A. nemorosa*, the wood anemone. All the species have beautifully formed, often downy foliage and "true" flowers: five or six petals with a prominent stamen center.

spring-flowering anemones

The low-growing, spring-flowering species all have pinnate, hairy foliage and, after flowering, striking, fluffy seed heads. The spring anemones are not spectacular, but they have a subtlety that gives you goose bumps. They often flower a second time in summer.

A. xlesseri

☀ ◑ ↕ 30 ✿ 5-6

Flowers profusely with unusual, carmine-pink blooms.

A. multifida

☀ ◑ ↕ 30 ✿ 5-6

Syn. *A. magellanica*. Flowers sulfur yellow.

A. sylvestris

☀ ◑ ↕ 30 ✿ 5-6

Cream colored. In spite of its scientific name (*sylvestris* means "from the woods"), this species differs from the previous two because it is a steppe plant that feels most at home in a dry, sunny situation. It even tends to become rampant there. Variety *macrantha* has larger flowers.

summer-flowering anemones

These anemones are larger and slightly coarser than their spring-flowering cousins but, even so, they still give you plenty of goose bumps.

A. cylindrica

☀ ◑ ↕ 120 ✿ 7-8

An extraordinary species with stiff, upright stems. The long-stemmed, greenish-white flowers, with their high green stamen centers, are pretty in themselves, and after flowering the centers lengthen into seed pods which are covered in silvery down.

A. leveillei

☀ ◑ ↕ 70 ✿ 5-7

Leaves have slightly shallower indentations than those on other anemones. The flowers are delightful: white with lilac blue on the underside and blue stamens.

autumn or Japanese anemones

These anemones, which are from China and Japan, flower last and grow the tallest. They all have large deeply cut foliage and airy racemes of relatively large flowers on long stems. All the autumn-flowering anemones must be protected during the first winter. Because there are countless cultivars, we describe only those we consider the most beautiful.

A. hupehensis

☀ ◑ ↕ 80-100 ✿ 8-9

Does not grow very tall, has leaves composed of three leaflets, and produces warm pink flowers.

'Crispa'
Syn. *A. xhybrida* 'Lady Gilmour'. Unusual, curled-up foliage. Very free-flowering.

'Hadspen Abundance'
Compact growth and deep pink-red flowers.

A. xhybrida
A group of hybrids of mixed parentage.

'Honorine Jobert'

☀ ◑ ↕ 130 ✿ 8-10

The most beautiful white Japanese anemone.

'Königin Charlotte'

☀ ◑ ↕ 120 ✿ 8-10

Semidouble, soft pink flowers with a deeper pink underside.

'Pamina'

☀ ◑ ↕ 80 ✿ 9-10

Low growing with semidouble, pinkish-red flowers.

'Whirlwind'

☀ ◑ ↕ 100 ✿ 8-10

Semidouble, white flowers. Grows slowly but is well worth waiting for.

A. tomentosa

☀ ◑ ↕ 120 ✿ 7-9

Large and less deeply cut foliage.
'Albadura'
Very light pink flowers and darker pink in bud.
'Robustissima'
Grows tall (150 cm), bears pale pink flowers, and becomes rampant on fertile soil.

Angelica, Apiaceae, angelica

Angelicas are robust umbellifers, just as impressive as the hogweeds (*Heracleum* species), but without the unpleasant habit of causing skin burns. They are recognizable by their domed and not flat flower heads. Short lived, but usually very good self-seeders, especially on rich, moisture-retentive soil.

A. gigas

☀ ◑ ↕ 140 ✿ 7-8

A magnificent species from Korea, with deep dark red flower heads. It could be the showpiece of every border were it not an unreliable self-seeder. So what to do? Buy new plants again?

A. sylvestris 'Vicar's Mead'

☀ ◑ ↕ 140 ✿ 7-8

A form of the common angelica with grayish-blue foliage, purple-flushed stems and leaf base, and pinkish flower heads.

Anthemis, Asteraceae, chamomile

A. xhybrida 'E. C. Buxton'

☀ ↕ 70 ✿ 6-10

An improvement on the well-known 'Wargrave Variety'. An amazing plant with palmate, chamomile foliage and a continuous show of soft yellow daisylike flowers with dark yellow centers. Unfortunately, they do not survive for long. Radical pruning in September (very painful because the plant is still in full flower) encourages flowering the following summer. Especially suitable for a quick impact in a first-year border or to fill gaps in an established border.

Aquilegia, Ranunculaceae, *columbine*

We remain enthusiastic about the buttercup family. Primitive or not, columbines are a miracle of design. Jan van Eyck and Albrecht Dürer, renowned 15th-century artists, thought so in their time and we still do: distinctive ternate, lobed leaves, often covered in a glaucous blue haze, and nodding flowers, with five colored sepals and five colored petals. The latter have an upward-pointing spur. Columbines generally only live for a few years but self-seed well, so you never need be without. A humus-rich soil and light shade are appreciated.

A. flabellata
☼ ☽ ↕ 30 ✿ 5-6

Syn. *A. akitensis.* A low-growing species with relatively large blue and white flowers. If it were possible to choose the most beautiful columbine (they are all beautiful), then it would be this one.

A. xhybrida 'Nora Barlow'
☼ ☽ ↕ 70 ✿ 5-6

Double, white flowers with smudges of white, red, and pink—absolutely delightful. Nothing wild about this double variety, but it would still look good in the wildest gardens. Repeats well from seed.

Aralia, Araliaceae

Besides the well-known Japanese angelica tree (*A. elata*), the genus *Aralia* consists of herbaceous plants that are undeservedly little known. They all have compound leaves (like an elder but far more attractive) and panicles of ivylike flowers, followed by blue-black berries. Although they grow best in semishade on fertile, moisture-retentive soil, they are remarkably strong and can tolerate poor soil, sun, and drought.

A. californica
☼ ☽ ↕ 300 ✿ 7-8

A huge plant that, given good soil, can easily reach 3 m in height and width. Gracefully nodding, greenish-white flower panicles are followed by black berries on purple stems. Fully hardy, although in the wild the plant does not grow farther north than the Siskiyou Mountains in southern Oregon. There it grows alongside another giant plant, *Darmera peltata*, in wet, well-shaded situations. An idea for the garden?

A. continentalis
☼ ☽ ↕ 200 ✿ 7-8

This species hails from Korea and is possibly even more beautiful than *A. californica*, although it does not grow as tall. The compound leaves grow just as large (up to 1.2 m). The greenish-white flower panicles turn to pink and are followed by enormous purple berries that hang down like bunches of grapes.

A. racemosa
☽ ↕ 100 ✿ 6-7

The smallest species in the genus. From eastern North America. Has cream-colored fluffy inflorescences and shiny black berries. Spreads steadily in light shade.

Artemisia, Asteraceae, *mugwort*

Oddly enough, mugwort species are seldom mentioned in older gardening books and, consequently, were not popular in the past. Recently, all has changed under the influence of various fashion trends prescribing borders in gray and white, gray and yellow, or gray and red. The extremely gray artemisias thereby became indispensable. In fashion or not, artemisias will remain popular in the future. The gray color that knits all the other colors together is far too attractive to fall out of favor again. All the species except *A. lactiflora* prefer dry, well-drained soil and plenty of sun. They suffer in very wet winters.

A. absinthium
☼ ↕ 80 ✿ 7-8

Being indigenous to temperate Europe, this is the easiest artemisia for that area. It is absolutely hardy and not prone to rotting in wet winters. Pruning plants before the longest day (be careful, not too far) postpones flowering, which is uninteresting anyway, and the plants remain compact. The beautifully compound foliage of **'Lambrook Silver'** is grayer than that of the other artemisias.

A. alba 'Canescens'
☼ ↕ 60 ✿ n/a

Threadlike, filigree-like gray foliage and elegant upward-reaching flower stems.

A. lactiflora
☼ ☽ ↕ 175 ✿ 8-9

An unusual species with glossy, dark green lobed foliage and large panicles full of cream-colored "pinheads." The plant definitely requires moisture-retentive soil and is absolutely intolerant of drought. Plants with purple-flushed young foliage and purple stems belong to the **Guizhou Group**, and *A. lactiflora* **Guizhou Group 'Rosa Schleier'** promises pink flowers as well.

A. ludoviciana var. latiloba
☼ ↕ 40 ✿ n/a

A coarse, slightly rampant plant. In places where it has sufficient space, for instance, between low shrubs, it can form a wonderful silvery white hummock. Although attractive brownish-gray flower spikes appear in June, we recommend cutting back the whole plant to 20 cm just before the flowers appear. This will prevent the plant from collapsing into disarray in summer, with all the stems tangled up together.

Aruncus, Rosaceae, *goat's beard*

A. 'Horatio'
☼ ☽ ↕ 120 ✿ 6-7

A breathtakingly beautiful cross between the familiar, immensely strong giant plant *A. dioicus* and the unsightly *A. aethusifolius*. The hybrid has attractive, compound, divided foliage that turns a beautiful color in autumn. It bears elegant panicles of cream-colored small flowers on reddish-brown stems.

Asarum, Aristolochiaceae, *wild ginger*

Slow-growing plants for deep shade and good woodland soil that does not dry out. Evergreen foliage. To see the curious, three-petaled brown flowers you will have to get down on your knees for they remain concealed under the leaves.

A. canadense
☽ ● ↕ 25 ✿ 3-4

Heart-shaped, velvety green leaves can reach 15 cm across.

Above
Anemone cylindrica

Far left
Amsonia tabernaemontana
var. *salicifolia*

Above left
Anemone tomentosa
'Robustissima'

Below left
Artemisia lactiflora
Guizhou Group 'Rosa
Schleier'; with the yellow
flowers of *Inula magnifica*
'Sonnenstrahl' behind.

Above
Aruncus 'Horatio'

Right
Aquilegia xhybrida
'Nora Barlow'

A. europaeum

◑ ● ↕ 15 ✿ 2-4

Kidney-shaped, glossy, dark green leaves with light green veins. The leaves reach 10 cm across.

Asclepias, Asclepiadaceae, *milk weed*

A. incarnata

☼ ↕ 140 ✿ 7

A sturdy border plant with umbel-shaped inflorescences covered in sweet-smelling, pale pink flowers, which are dark red in bud. The flowers attract many insects and are followed by attractive, upright, pointed seed heads. There is also a white-flowering form, '**Alba**'.

Asphodeline, Asphodelaceae, *Jacob's rod*

A. lutea

☼ ↕ 100 ✿ 5-6

Grassy, blue-gray leaf rosettes appear in autumn and die down after the flowering period. The tall flower spikes, which only appear in warm, sunny spots (the plant hails from southern Europe) are covered from top to bottom with wispy, bright yellow starlike flowers. Seed capsules as big as marbles follow the flowers.

Aster, Asteraceae

Since time immemorial we have been confronted with those terrible lilac-purple asters in garden after garden after garden, while so many other aster species were ignored, some of them very beautiful. Asters are strong plants that thrive almost anywhere. They should be divided every three or four years in spring, otherwise the clumps will become too big and the outside flower stalks will collapse. Division is easy, which explains why we see whole streets with just one species of aster in every garden.

A. amellus

☼ ↕ 40-60 ✿ 7-10

Comparatively large spectacular flowers. The ordinary species easily collapses, but the cultivars listed here are reasonably sturdy.
'**Rose Erfüllung**'
Pink rays and yellow centers.
'**Sonora**'
Dark purple rays and yellow centers.

A. cordifolius

☼ ↕ 100 ✿ 9-10

A bushy plant with clouds of small violet-blue flowers late in autumn. Banishes all the autumn blues. Unfortunately, rather prone to disease; then the lower leaves, and sometimes even a number of the stems, die off early. However, between other tall plants this is not noticeable and the flowers, which always put in an appearance, are too beautiful to ignore. The hybrid '**Little Carlow**' is, in our experience, the healthiest.

A. divaricatus

☼ ◑ ↕ 60 ✿ 7-9

A remarkable species that tolerates an amazing amount of drought and shade. Modest white flower heads appear when hardly anything else can be found in a shaded garden.

A. ericoides 'Blue Star'

☼ ↕ 60 ✿ 8-10

A compact aster that tolerates drought. It has narrow, heatherlike foliage and clouds of pale blue aster flowers.

A. x frikartii 'Mönch'

☼ ↕ 70 ✿ 7-10

An infertile cross with comparatively large violet-blue flowers with yellow centers. The plant flowers endlessly until deep into the autumn. This plant has been around for a very long time but we just had to mention it—it is so beautiful!

A. laevis

☼ ↕ 160 ✿ 9-10

A wonderful, tall species with elongated bunches of pale violet-blue flowers. One of the most attractive wild asters.

A. lateriflorus 'Horizontalis'

☼ ↕ 60 ✿ 8-10

A bushy-growing plant, like a small shrub. Free-flowering white blooms with reddish centers above dark foliage. The foliage color ensures that the plant is always attractive, even when not in flower. It is so beautiful. Will it appear in garden after garden after garden? There are worse scenarios imaginable.

A. macrophyllus

☼ ◑ ↕ 80 ✿ 7-9

A coarse plant with broad leaves and lilac-colored flowers that tolerates a great deal of shade and drought. This last quality has been passed on to a hybrid (with *A. amellus*?): '**Twilight**' is not coarse and it blooms over a long period, with blue flowers and yellow centers turning to red.

A. novae-angliae

☼ ↕ 125 ✿ 8-10

From the dreadful aster mentioned in our introduction to this species, some lovely cultivars have emerged, such as '**Andenken an Alma Pötschke**' with carmine-pink flowers, '**Septemberrubin**' with ruby-red flowers, and '**Violetta**' with deep purple flowers. Butterflies love all three.

A. umbellatus

☼ ◑ ↕ 180 ✿ 9-10

A tall rampant plant, with unusual inflorescences; the creamy white flowers are grouped into flat umbels. Not very striking at first sight but still an important (sturdy) plant for the back of the border. This extremely strong plant will thrive anywhere. It even survives among stinging nettles. The winter silhouette is beautiful.

Aster hybrids

'**Anja's Choice**'

☼ ↕ 120 ✿ 9-10

A free-flowering, sturdy plant, with clouds of small lilac-pink flowers whose centers turn red.
'**Herfstweelde**'

☼ ↕ 140 ✿ 9-11

Similar to *A. ericoides*, but twice as tall. The stems bend under the weight of the huge panicles of light blue flowers.
'**Oktoberlicht**'

☼ ↕ 160 ✿ 9-11

The medium-sized flowers are white and the centers turn reddish brown. A wide-spreading plant.

Astilbe, Saxifragaceae

Plants with beautiful pinnate leaves and panicles of flowers that look a little like spirea, which is why they are often misnamed. True spiraeas are shrubs and belong to the rose family. Among the popular assortment are some plants with garish colors (white, pink, or red). These are extremely difficult to incorporate into a garden. Moreover, they have a shallow root system and are, therefore, real thirsty fellows. Even the slightest lack of water makes their leaves curl up and turn brown.

A. chinensis var. taquetii 'Purpurlanze'

☼ ◐ ↕ 100 ✾ 7-8

A stiff, upright plant with a 30-cm-long, lightly branched, purple inflorescence. Spreads well but is not rampant. Especially useful as an architectural plant, in winter too, because the plant remains attractive after flowering. Tolerates more drought than the other astilbes.

A. simplicifolia

☼ ◐ ↕ 30-50 ✾ 7-8

A dainty plant with decorative, dark, shiny foliage, dark leaf stems, and loose sprays of flowers in pastel shades. Suitable for planting in large groups between taller plants.

'Dunkellachs'
Dark salmon-pink flowers above shiny, dark green foliage.

'Sprite'
Resembles the previous plant but the flowers are a slightly deeper shade of pink

A. thunbergii 'Prof. van der Wielen'

☼ ◐ ↕ 120 ✾ 8-9

A tall white-flowering species with an elegant, airy inflorescence. Looks like goat's beard (Aruncus) but flowers much later in the season.

Astilboides, Saxifragaceae, astilboides

☼ ◐ ↕ 120 ✾ 6-7

A. tabularis

Syn. Rodgersia tabularis. A beautiful foliage plant with huge, fresh green "saucers" on thick, hairy stems. An absolute attention seeker of the first order, suitable for architectural purposes. The tall flower stems, with small cream-colored flowers, are an added attraction. Moisture-retentive soil is important.

Astrantia, Apiaceae, masterwort

Delightful, old-fashioned plants that are once more back in fashion, and rightly so. Attractive, glossy and shallowly indented foliage. The "flowers" are subtly colored bracts (called involucres with umbels), within which the true,

umbel-shaped flower can be seen. All species like fertile, moisture-retentive soil.

A. major

☼ ◐ ↕ 60 ✾ 5-9

The involucre of the ordinary species is 3 cm large with numerous, smooth-edged leaflets in white with smudges of green and pink. The most important cultivars are mentioned here.

'Claret'
Deep, dark red flowers.

'Roma'
Strong, antique-rose-colored flowers.

'Washfield'
Flower color somewhere between the dark red 'Claret' and the antique rose 'Roma'.

A. major subsp. involucrata

☼ ◐ ↕ 80 ✾ 5-9

In all aspects larger than the species. It has slightly fringed involucral bracts.

'Canneman'
A plant with large flowers first discovered by the late Mrs. Canneman in her garden near Walbrzych, Poland. This sturdy plant comes into flower early (from the end of April onwards) with large red blooms that gradually turn to green. It often flowers a second time in summer.

'Shaggy'
A green and white flowering cultivar, also known under the name **'Margery Fish'**. The involucral bracts are elongated strips.

A. maxima

☼ ◐ ↕ 60 ✾ 6-7

The three-lobed foliage is larger than that of A. major, and the plant is slightly invasive. The involucral bracts have a fascinating color that is difficult to describe: we think velvety, shell-pink sounds attractive. Have you a garden on clay soil? Well, give this one a try.

Baptisia, Fabaceae, false indigo

Such wonderful plants, it seems unfair that they are relatively unknown. They look a little like lupins (they are related) but have far more verve. The plants reach a ripe old age but take some time to become established. They turn black in autumn.

B. australis

☼ ↕ 120 ✾ 6

The strong stems bear bluish-green leaves and truly indigo blue flowers. These are followed by fat, gray-green pods which remain into the autumn. A dry climate and plenty of sunshine are good for this plant.

B. lactea

☼ ↕ 140 ✾ 6-7

Strong gray stems push up through the soil like asparagus. The plant bears gray buds and white flowers. Tolerates slightly damper soil than does B. australis. A slow grower.

B. 'Purple Smoke'

☼ ↕ 100 ✾ 5-6

A hybrid between B. alba and B. australis. Purple-blue flowers and stems are covered in a smoky haze of anthracite.

Borago, Boraginaceae, borage

☼ ◐ ↕ 20 ✾ 6-7

B. pygmaea

Syn. B. laxiflora. This perennial is far different from the well-known annual kitchen herb B. offi-cinalis. From within a rosette of roughly haired, knobbly leaves, tall spindly stems arise, topped with an unfurling flash of heavenly blue, star-shaped flowers, which are about 1 1/2 cm across. The unfurling continues throughout the summer, so a few flowers are open at all times. By the end of summer the stems can reach up to 1 m in height and will have wormed their way through all the surrounding plants. The plant does not tolerate very severe frosts but self-seeds well.

Calamintha, Lamiaceae, calamint

A genus of aromatic garden plants closely related to thyme and mint. The most important feature is the long flower stem, on which an airy inflorescence is formed.

C. grandiflora

☼ ◐ ↕ 35 ✾ 5-8

Syn. Satureja grandiflora. This calamint from central Europe, with comparatively large lilac-pink-lipped flowers, has the pleasant quality of continuing to flower throughout the summer. An important garden plant that blends in easily with other colors.

Left
Asphodeline lutea

Below
Aster amellus 'Rosa Erfüllung' with *Anemone xhybrida* 'Honorine Jobert'

Bottom
Red admiral butterfly (*Vanessa atalanta*) on *Aster novae-angliae* 'Violetta'; with *Helianthus* 'Lemon Queen' behind

Above
Astrantia maxima

Right
Astrantia major subsp.
involucrata
'Canneman'

C. nepeta subsp. nepeta

☼ ↕ 30 ✿ 7-10

Syn. *C. nepetoides*. If there is one plant that smells of peppermint, this is it. You cannot help wanting to touch it. Low plants for a sunny spot. They have small blue-green leaves and endlessly flowering "clouds" of pale blue-lipped flowers. If '**Alba**' is written behind the name, then the flowers are pure white.

Campanula, Campanulaceae, *bellflower*

From way back, dozens of species of bellflower have been grown as garden plants. And rightly so, for they are all beautiful. Here are a few favorite species.

C. lactiflora

☼ ◐ ↕ 150 ✿ 6-8

A bellflower that flowers longer than most of the other species, does not collapse, and produces gigantic sprays of hundreds of flowers in colors that vary from purple-blue to pink At least this applies to the wild form that, amazingly enough, is rarely grown. Numerous cultivars have been produced, including some dwarf.

'Loddon Anna'
A tall cultivar with very pale pink flowers. Seedlings revert back to the wild species.

C. latiloba

☼ ◐ ↕ 80 ✿ 6-7

Closely related to the familiar peach-leaved bellflower (*C. persicifolia*), but differs in that the wide-open star-shaped flowers grow stiffly against the spikes. The result is a wonderful lilac-blue torch. Should be divided every few years to encourage profuse flowering.

'Alba'
Produces white flowers.

'Hidcote Amethyst'
Lilac-pink flowers.

Campanula hybrids

Several hybrids of *C. punctata*, an invasive species from Asia, and *C. takesimana*, a species of little attraction, and a few European species seed abundantly. The surprising outcome is a number of spectacular, large-flowered plants which are neither invasive nor self-seeding and, moreover, flower for a second time in late summer. Good on dry soil.

'Burghaltii'

☼ ↕ 50 ✿ 6-7

The lax stems with rather untidy foliage bear fascinating, aubergine-colored buds. Afterwards, pendulous, 5-cm-long bellflowers appear in a color that can best be described as lilac-gray. The plant requires a bit of work (support) but it is well worth it.

'Kent Belle'

☼ ◐ ↕ 100 ✿ 6-7

Similar to 'Burghaltii' but produces dark purple-blue flowers and tends to spread, although you cannot consider it invasive. Found by Elizabeth Strangman.

'Sarastro'

☼ ◐ ↕ 80 ✿ 6-7

Found by Christian Kress of Austria. It bears large flowers that are deep purple-blue like 'Kent Blue', but it has stronger stems.

Cardamine, Brassicaceae, *meadow cress*

C. waldsteinii

◐ ● ↕ 20 ✿ 4-5

A fresh spring plant that forms clumps of compound, rather angular foliage and is covered in heaps of large white lady's smock flowers. Once it has flowered it disappears underground again.

Centaurea, Asteraceae, *knapweed*

A large genus of plants with many hundreds of different species, especially in southern Europe. You very rarely see them in gardens, which is strange when you consider their wonderful flowers. Instead of a detailed description of the flowers, we refer you to the cornflower, which is a *Centaurea* species, because the flowers of all the species, whatever their color, look similar.

C. benoistii

☼ ↕ 100 ✿ 7-8

A fast-growing plant with grayish-green, deeply cut leaves and small burgundy-red flowers. Somewhat lax and floppy during flowering, but it is so beautiful, we have to forgive it.

C. glastifolia

☼ ↕ 100 ✿ 7-8

A large well-branched plant with elongated leaves and a dome-shaped pale yellow flower head above a golden-brown bract. The plant originates in the Ukraine and radiates from warmth, sun, and the south.

C. montana

☼ ◐ ↕ 40 ✿ 5-6

The mountain knapweed, with its large blue cornflowers poised above gray foliage, has been a well-known garden plant for centuries. We are including the species in this book to draw attention to '**Carnea**', with its enchantingly beautiful, pale lilac-pink flowers and dark lilac-purple stamens. After flowering in May to June, the plant continues to produce a few flowers throughout the summer.

C. 'Pulchra Major'

☼ ↕ 120 ✿ 6-7

An impressive plant with large lobed, gray foliage and lilac-pink flowers on tall, sturdy stems. The flowers are enclosed in large paper-like bracts. Not an easy customer: the plant requires a heavy soil (clay) that must not become waterlogged in winter.

Cephalaria, Dipsacaceae

C. dipsacoides

☼ ↕ 180 ✿ 7-8

Not as tall as *C. gigantea* and blooming later with small pale yellow, button-shaped flowers.

C. gigantea

☼ ◐ ↕ 250 ✿ 6-7

A huge plant with a subtle, lightly branched inflorescence full of lemon yellow *Scabiosa*-like flowers above rather large coarsely indented foliage. Because of its airy appearance, it is also suitable for planting between medium-tall plants. In the wild (in the Caucasus) it grows alongside *Campanula lactiflora*: that must be a wonderful sight (in the garden too)! The plants do not collapse when grown in soil that is not very wet. *Cephalaria alpina* '**Nana**' also does not collapse, for it remains much shorter.

Ceratostigma, Plumbaginaceae, *plumbago*

C. plumbaginoides

☼ ◐ ↕ 25 ✿ 9-10

A beautiful plant for the foreground with regularly shaped, gentian blue flowers (just as they are always drawn with five small petals) that burst forth from brushlike, red-flushed flower heads. As the flowers appear the foliage turns an attractive red autumn color. You could not dream up anything quite so beautiful!

Chamaenerion see *Epilobium*

Chrysanthemum see *Dendranthema, Leucanthemella,* and *Tanacetum*

Cimicifuga see *Actaea*

Cirsium, Asteraceae, *plumed thistle*

C. rivulare 'Atropurpureum'

☼ ↕ 120 ❋ 5-9

A nonprickly, real thistle with wonderful purple-red flower heads. A strong plant with attractive, dentate foliage. 'Atropurpureum' is an old plant that had almost disappeared but has survived in the Mien Ruys gardens in eastern Netherlands, and from there has come onto the market again. Sterile (so does not self-seed) and long-flowering but it must be taken up every other year and divided to keep it flourishing. The wild species belongs to a group of nonprickly thistles that brighten up European and Asian hay marshes with eye-catching flowers. It is often seen growing there alongside *Iris sibirica*. A sublime combination for the garden, too.

Clematis, Ranunculaceae, *old man's beard, clematis*

Alongside the dozens of well-known and lesser-known climbing plants, there are also a few perennial *Clematis* species, the stems of which never, or rarely, become woody and they shoot up through the soil every spring. However, they do not deny their origins: they cannot stand on their own feet. They have to be supported by canes or better (and easier) still, by surrounding low shrubs or sturdy perennials. But then they are exquisite beauties. Rich, limey soil is appreciated.

C. heracleifolia 'China Purple'

☼ ◐ ↕ 100 ❋ 8-10

Forms a sturdy, bushy plant with perfumed, dark purple-blue flowers that strongly resemble hyacinths.

C. integrifolia

☼ ◐ ↕ 80 ❋ 6-7

A delightful species that should be allowed to grow as it pleases among the surrounding perennials: in this way it will manage to climb up high. It has pretty, oval leaves and large dark blue, slightly pendulous bell-shaped flowers with cream-colored centers. On top of all that, the plant has attractive, fluffy seed heads. For someone seeing it for the first time, it is a sensational plant.
'Alba'
White flowers.
'Rosea'
Pink flowers.

C. x jouiniana 'Praecox'

☼ ◐ ↕ 250 ❋ 7-9

From a woody base, long stems, which must be supported, appear annually. Can also be used as ground cover. Pale blue flowers in large sprays.
'Mrs Robert Brydon'
Longer stems and flowers a little later in loose sprays.

C. recta

☼ ◐ ↕ 200 ❋ 6-8

This plant definitely needs support from low shrubs or tall perennials (for example, monkshood species), otherwise it turns into chaos. Planted in the correct way it is a wonder to behold with attractive, deeply cut foliage and clouds of cream-colored flowers that smell delightful. These are followed by decorative seed "tails."
'Purpurea'
Even more beautiful than the species. The foliage and stems are tinged with purple in spring.

Codonopsis, Campanulaceae

C. clematidea

☼ ◐ ↕ 60 ❋ 7-8

The strongest and most easily obtainable species of the Asian counterpart of the mainly European genus *Campanula*. There are dozens of species, some of them climbers, which are, however, rather weak for our climate (and fall prey to snails and slugs). *Codonopsis clematidea*, though, is a strong, easy plant with large delicate blue, bell-shaped flowers. On the inside the plant has an improbably intricate mosaic design in chocolate, orange, and green. If possible, plant it high enough that you can look into it from beneath while you are sitting down (or even standing up). Humus-rich soil is important.

Coreopsis, Asteraceae, *tick seed*

C. tripteris

☼ ↕ 250 ❋ 9-10

An attractive species of the common, rather stiff-looking tick seed, suitable for wilder situations. In spite of its height it does not collapse. Slender stems with rosettes of narrow foliage and racemes of small yellow sunflowers with brown centers.

Crambe, Brassicaceae, *sea kale*

Giant plants with enormous leaves and huge inflorescences. These superlatives are necessary, for everything about this plant is excessive. Chalky soil is important to prevent club root, a typical cabbage disease. The link with cabbage is obvious from the fact that the caterpillars of the cabbage white butterfly feast on *Crambe*, too.

C. cordifolia

☼ ↕ 180 ❋ 6

Enormous, heart-shaped, puckered leaves and a raceme of thousands of small white, four-petaled flowers that have an unusual smell. Clearly a "must have" plant. We shall just have to put up with the disadvantages: some years it forgets to flower, which results in a big gap in the border, and the flowers are so large that they can easily snap off in a strong wind. When strong winds are forecast in June the plant should, as a preventative measure, be supported by bamboo canes.

C. maritima

☼ ↕ 50 ❋ 6

The wild sea kale of our coastal sands. In all its aspects it is smaller than the previous species and extremely wind resistant. The puckered, fleshy foliage is pure bluish gray and unique to behold. The flower "hummocks," with their hundreds of white flowers, complete the picture. A plant for dry weather and a burning sun.

Darmera, Saxifragaceae

D. peltata

☼ ◐ ↕ 70 ❋ 4-5

A foliage plant for around the pond or on damp soil; it has huge, slightly puckered, round leaves. Looks a little like butter bur (*Petasites hybridus*) but the plant is not invasive (although it spreads slowly through its rhizomes). The leaves are snail- and slug-proof in summer and die off in autumn in fabulous shades of red and orange. Before the leaves appear in spring, the plant bears pink, semicircular flower heads on strong stems.

Top
Artemisia lactiflora Guizhou Group 'Rosa Schleier' (left) and *Campanula lactiflora* (right). In the background *Monarda* 'Squaw'.

Above
The pale yellow knot-like flowers of *Cephalaria gigantea* in a classical combination with *Campanula lactiflora*. In front, the slender spikes of *Veronicastrum virginicum* 'Lavendelturm'.

Center left
Campanula 'Burghaltii'

Left
Centaurea glastifolia

Top
Cirsium rivulare
'Atropurpureum' with
Geranium pratense

Above
Coreopsis tripteris

Right
Clematis integrifolia

Datisca, Datiscaceae

D. cannabina

☼ ↕ 180 ✿ 7-8

Strongly resembles the hemp plant but is unrelated and also has no intoxicating effects. A slender plant with small greenish-yellow flowers on long, arching stems.

Delphinium, Ranunculaceae, *delphinium*

Perhaps delphiniums should not be included in this book. Because of their gigantic, top-heavy inflorescences, which easily collapse, and the riot of color which they produce, it is almost impossible to combine them with other plants, as the trend towards more natural gardening dictates. True, some new forms have once more appeared on the market during the past few years, but this has been an ongoing process for a century. They are more suited to the Victorian Age, when a plant had to be admired from all sides. That the delphiniums were propped up all round by "scaffolding" was not considered a disadvantage and, moreover, gardeners to do all this work cost next to nothing in those days. So why delphiniums in this book? Because every time we see delphiniums we are struck dumb by all that riot of blue and are inspired (post modern) to do something beautiful with them: for instance, combine them with grasses or other less eye-catching, flowering plants. A handy tip: cut them back before they are in full flower, then they will not collapse and a second, stronger flowering will follow. They are all at their best on rich, fertile, preferably clay soil. They require an annual dressing of bone meal. From the many hundreds of examples we have made the following, purely personal, selection.

D. elatum

☼ ↕ 180 ✿ 6-7

The wild delphinium that still appears occasionally in the mountains of central Europe. Stronger than most of the cultivars. Bears blue or purple flowers on slender spikes.

D. ×belladonna hybrids

Of medium height. After cutting back, this hybrid flowers for a second time with a few blooms.

'Casa Blanca'
No more than 80 cm tall and bears white flowers.

'Cliveden Beauty'
Reaches 120 cm and bears big, sky-blue flowers.

Delphinium hybrids and cultivars

'Astolat'
A sowing breed with enormous, almost top-heavy racemes full of loose, floppy flowers. The color is lilac pink with a white or light brown "bee." The first flowers are best off in a vase, so that a second, more compact flowering can form. Height up to 180 cm.

'Berghimmel'
One of the most famous cultivars from Karl Foerster, this plant has an open inflorescence with large heavenly blue flowers and white eyes. The buds are steel blue and the plant reaches 180 cm in height.

'Black Knight'
Reaches 180 cm tall with dark violet flowers with black eyes.

'Cameliard'
Growing 180 cm tall with thick spikes of lavender-blue flowers.

'Galahad'
Also 180 cm tall with white flowers on tall spikes.

'Lanzenträger'
Up to 2 m in height with 80-cm-tall, slender spikes full of gentian blue flowers with white eyes.

'Zauberflöte'
A large part of the 160-cm-tall plant is taken up by the long, well-branched raceme full of clear blue flowers with a striking white eye.

Dendranthema, Asteraceae, *chrysanthemum*

D. 'Anja's Bouquet'
D. 'Herbstbrokat'
D. 'Paul Boissier'

☼ ↕ 70-100 ✿ 10-11

These are what you call chrysanthemums, such as you buy at the florist's, but with far smaller flowers and completely hardy. Flowering occurs late, sometimes too late, when there are severe night frosts in October, but it is most charming. 'Anja's Bouquet' is pink, 'Herbstbrokat' reddish brown, and 'Paul Boissier' rather lanky but stunning orange.

Dianthus, Caryophyllaceae, *carnation, pink*

Many species belong in this genus of sun- and drought-loving plants, all with grasslike foliage and small flowers in pastel colors. Most of the species are plants for enthusiasts, who are prepared to give them the care and attention they require (panes of glass, winter cover, and so forth). We shall describe a few of the stronger species.

D. amurensis

☼ ↕ 30 ✿ 7-9

The comparatively large flowers of this species have a most unusual color for a pink: lilac blue.

D. carthusianorum

☼ ↕ 60 ✿ 6-8

The Carthusian pink has long stems, narrow foliage, and sweet William-like clusters of small hard pink flowers. It is long-living and also profusely self-seeding on dry, chalky places.

D. sanguineus

☼ ↕ 50 ✿ 6-8

A local variant of the Carthusian pink from Slovenia, with blood-red flowers.

Dictamnus, Rutaceae, *burning bush*

D. albus

☼ ↕ 70 ✿ 6-7

A slow-growing but long-lived plant, with a robust spike of curiously shaped, pale pink flowers veined in lilac and with beautiful, prickly seeds. It thrives best in a warm spot on well-drained soil. Both the flowers and the seeds produce an ethereal oil that, on warm summer days, crackles like fireworks if you hold a light to them. Some people are susceptible to skin burns if they come into touch with them, so be careful. In wet summers the snails and slugs will gobble the whole plant up but in a drier summer it will grow again. Do not transplant—it will never recover.

'Albiflorus'
Pure white flowers.

Digitalis, Scrophulariaceae, *foxglove*

Foxgloves are biennials or short-lived perennials that self-seed profusely. From a rosette of leaves that is formed in the first year, a flower stem grows in the following year, sometimes branched, which is thickly covered with drooping, thimblelike flowers. After flowering the plants usually die off.

D. ferruginea

The tall, somewhat branched flower stem is laden with beige flowers, veined with brown on the inside. One of the most beautiful and effective plants that we know. Because the leaf rosettes remain green during the winter, light winter protection is advised during a long period of frost.

D. grandiflora
☼ ◑ ↕ 60 ✽ 7-8

Syn. *D. ambigua*. Resembles the familiar foxglove, but does not grow as tall and bears attractive, soft yellow flowers that have brown veins. The foliage is clearly less hairy. This species is the most permanent of all the foxgloves, especially on soil that is deficient in lime.

D. lutea
☼ ◑ ↕ 60 ✽ 7-8

A short-lived plant with long, narrow, hairless, glossy green foliage and long racemes of small greenish yellow "thimbles." Self-seeds profusely.

D. xmertonensis
☼ ◑ ↕ 50 ✽ 7-8

Seems to be an improved specimen of the ordinary foxglove. Large subtle pinkish-red flowers are borne above large shiny, slightly hairy foliage. Protect against too much dampness in winter.

D. parviflora
☼ ◑ ↕ 60 ✽ 6-7

The stems are covered from top to bottom with minute, chocolate-brown flowers. Wonderful between *Deschampsia caespitosa*.

Echinacea, Asteraceae, *cone flower*

Sturdy plants from the North American prairie with spectacular, large daisylike flowers with a distinctive high "cone" center. They thrive in full sun on rich, well-drained soil.

E. pallida
☼ ↕ 100 ✽ 7-9

Narrow leaves and narrow, purplish-pink petals that are folded back.

E. paradoxa
☼ ↕ 80 ✽ 7-9

Narrow, yellow-petaled flowers. The roots were used by American Indians to cure sore throats and to alleviate toothaches.

E. purpurea
☼ ↕ 80 ✽ 7-9

Syn. *Rudbeckia purpurea*. A sturdy plant with coarse, lance-shaped foliage and large spectacular flowers: a wreath of pinkish-red flower rays round an orange-brown cone-shaped disc. Besides being a superior type of border plant and a butterfly tempter, the plant is exceptionally useful: it provides a strong, natural antibiotic. While chewing on a few seeds you will notice that your tongue becomes numb.
'Augustkönigin'
Large flat lilac-pink flowers.
'Green Edge'
White flowers with a trace of green.
'Jade'
White flowers with green centers.
'Magnus'
Large horizontal flowers.
'Rubinglow'
Grows true from seed. It has exceptionally pretty shades of red petals.
'Rubinstern'
A cultivar with tapering leaves and with flowers that are redder than those 'Rubinglow'.
'Vintage Wine'
Must be propagated vegetatively. The flowers are, as the name promises, clear wine red.
'White Lustre'
The ordinary, white-flowering variety with folded-back petals.

Echinops, Asteraceae, *globe thistle*

Stately plants with deeply cut, more or less prickly leaves and large spherical flower heads at the top of a single, or a lightly branched, stem. Bees, bumblebees, and butterflies avidly visit the flowers. The plants thrive easily on dry or wet, poor or rich soil. Many species resemble each other somewhat, so the nomenclature is in a bit of a mess. We shall do our best.

E. bannaticus
☼ ◑ ↕ 160 ✽ 7-8

A sturdy plant with purple-blue flower heads that can reach up to 8 cm.

E. exaltatus
☼ ◑ ↕ 180 ✽ 7-8

A tall species with flower heads that are silver gray until just before flowering. In flower they are covered with a hint of blue.

E. ritro 'Veitch's Blue'
☼ ↕ 100 ✽ 7-8

A short species with vicious, 1 1/2-cm-long prickles and foliage that is white downy on the underside, as are the flower stems and the 3-cm-large deep-blue flower heads. 'Veitch's Blue' grows taller and has larger, equally blue flowers without vicious prickles.

E. sphaerocephalus
☼ ◑ ↕ 200 ✽ 7-8

The most widely available species (with all kinds of fanciful? names). The well-branched blue gray flower heads easily collapse but self-seed profusely. Especially suitable for wild gardens.

Echium, Boraginaceae, *viper's bugloss*

E. russicum
☼ ↕ 60 ✽ 6-7

The first year this biennial species forms a rosette of bumpy, rough-haired leaves from which a large compact, torchlike inflorescence of deep dark red flowers appears the following year. Grows in the wild in southern Russia, together with stipas and the lemon yellow *Allium obliquum*. Seeds well on rich, well-drained soil.

Epilobium, Onagraceae, *willow herb*

E. angustifolium
☼ ◑ ↕ 150 ✽ 6-8

Syn. *Chamaenerion angustifolium*. Willow herb is such a common plant that hardly anyone sees just how beautiful it really is. But one does notice the pure-white flowering form 'Album', which bears more (and possibly whiter) flowers than the wild form, and 'Stahl Rose', with its pale pink flowers enclosed in darker bracts. They are just as invasive as the wild form, especially on acid soil, but you can always dig up the rhizomes and eat them with a garlic dressing (reputed to be delicious).

Epimedium, Berberidaceae, *barrenwort, bishop's hat*

Ground-covering plants with wonderful, ternate foliage and small four-petaled flowers in spring. You will have to get down on your knees to see the flowers–and then remain breathlessly transfixed for half an hour–so beautiful. The main ornamental value is, however, the foliage that in almost all the species

Below
Dendranthema
'Herbstbrokat'

Bottom
Dianthus sanguineus
in Slovenia

Right
Dendranthema 'Paul
Boissier'

Above left
Digitalis parviflora

Left
Small tortoiseshell butterflies (*Vanessa urticae*) on *Echinops sphaerocephalus*

Above right
Epilobium angustifolium 'Stahl Rose'

Above
Echinacea purpurea 'Jade'

remains effective throughout the winter: it keeps its green color or turns an attractive brown or bronze shade. Cut off the old leaves in March, otherwise you will not see the flowers at all - and they are truly exceptional.

E. grandiflorum
◐ ● ↕ 25 ✿ 4-5

Syn. *E. macranthum*. Has the largest flowers of all; they can be 2–3 cm across. Color varies from white to lilac with streaks of white. The foliage disappears in winter. The flowers are clearly visible above the bronze-colored, sprouting leaves.
'Lilac Seedling'
As the name suggests, the flowers are lilac colored. They also are noticeably larger than those of the species.

E. xperralchicum 'Frohnleiten'
◐ ● ↕ 30 ✿ 4-5

A ground-covering plant with runners. Bears small pale yellow flowers and dark red, brown-mottled foliage that remains on the plant in winter. Tolerates more dryness than the other species.

E. xrubrum
◐ ● ↕ 25 ✿ 4-5

Small red flowers with white spurs and bronze-green young foliage. The old foliage turns brown in winter and remains on the plant. Cut off in March.

E. xversicolor 'Sulphureum'
◐ ● ↕ 25 ✿ 4-5

Both the winter foliage and the young, fresh leaves that emerge in spring are red. The flowers are sulfur yellow.

E. xyoungianum
◐ ● ↕ 20 ✿ 4-5

Fragile plants with bronze-brown new foliage in spring and sparkling flowers. The foliage disappears in winter.
'Niveum'
Flowers white.
'Roseum'
Flowers pink.

Eryngium, Apiaceae, *sea holly*

Unusual members of the umbellifer family in that the flowers are not in umbel-shaped inflorescences but are crammed together in thimble-like heads. The ordinary leaves and the involucral bracts are often dentate and prickly. All parts of the plants are in varying shades of steel blue. The well-known blue sea holly is an *Eryngium* species. Chalky soil is a requisite for healthy growth and flowering.

E. alpinum
☼ ↕ 70 ✿ 6-7

One of the most famous alpine plants, portrayed in all alpine flora books, but all but disappeared in the wild. (That is what happens when you are so beautiful, you get dug up!) Fresh green rosettes of dentate leaves and large elongated flower heads surrounded by fibrous, steel-blue involucral bracts. At its most beautiful as a solitary plant or at the front of the border, so that it can be admired from all sides. Now if you feel tempted to dig up the last wild specimen, please refrain from doing so, because the plant is widely available and easy to grow from seed.

E. bourgatii
☼ ↕ 60 ✿ 6-7

A Pyrenean species with deeply cut, gray-green leaves, veined in white, and several blue-green flower heads surrounded by lance-shaped involucral bracts. The flower stems are also blue.

E. giganteum
☼ ↕ 60 ✿ 6-8

A biennial with broad, silver-gray leaves and elongated, silver-blue inflorescences. The plant is a profuse self-seeder, and that is really nice, because it fits in anywhere and everywhere. After flowering gloriously the plant dies just as gloriously (in a shade of brown-black).

E. xtripartitum
☼ ↕ 60 ✿ 7-9

A perennial with a glossy, dark green rosette of leaves. The many richly branched flower stems bear hundreds of steel-blue flower heads and form mounds.

E. yuccifolium
☼ ↕ 100 ✿ 7-9

In the winter this species forms evergreen rosettes of sword-shaped, gray-green leaves covered with fine spines, just like *Yucca* species. Produces towards the end of summer greenish-white flower heads on lightly branched spikes. Attractive with grasses.

Eupatorium, Asteraceae, *common agrimony*

Large plants with coarse foliage and large umbels of flowers in late summer. All the species attract masses of butterflies and bees. Although they are really plants that feel at home on damp, fertile soil, they are so strong that they have to be practically ill-treated before they show signs of poor growth. After a number of years, clumps of these extremely robust plants become so large that the outer stems flop and topple over. To prevent this, divide the plants from time to time.

E. cannabinum
☼ ◐ ↕ 160 ✿ 7-9

Hemp agrimony is a coarse, thick-foliaged plant with divided, hemplike leaves and fluffy, pale pink umbels of flowers. It tends to seed overenthusiastically.
'Album'
White flowers so beautiful that you just have to put up with the plant's self-seeding aspect.
'Plenum'
Flowers double, in an unusual shade of old rose. The cultivar is sterile and does not self-seed.

E. maculatum
☼ ☼ ↕ 160-250 ✿ 7-9

The wild species, Joe Pye weed, is not unattractive—but no more than that. However, there are a few spectacular cultivars.
'Album'
The tallest cultivar, with white flowers that fade to brown. Very robust, never collapses.
'Atropurpureum'
The purple stems bear gigantic, purple-pink umbels that are so top-heavy the plant bends under the weight. Quite an awesome plant.
'Purple Bush'
Resembles 'Atropurpureum' but not as tall and bears compound panicles of flowers on far smaller umbels.

E. rugosum
☼ ☼ ↕ 120 ✿ 8-9

This plant seems coarse and uninteresting (stinging-nettlelike foliage) until it comes into flower, and then the fluffiness of the gray-white umbels, gives it an aura of delicacy. Delightful when combined with the later species of monkshood.
'Chocolate'
An interesting plant even before the flowers appear because of (as you will have guessed) the chocolate-colored foliage.

'Snowball'
Pure white flowers.

Euphorbia, Euphorbiaceae, *spurge*

A large genus of plants with thousands of representatives in the Old World. They can range from minute annuals or dwarfs from the higher alps, to viciously thorned bushes of bottle-shaped, cactuslike plants or huge trees. They all have two things in common: the "flowers" consist of two, attractively colored bracts (the actual flowers are inconspicuous), and the stems contain an extremely poisonous milk, which can be dangerous if it comes into contact with the eyes. Most of the species grow in the tropics and the subtropics and are, therefore, not hardy in our climate. However, among those that are hardy are some very attractive plants.

E. amygdaloides var. *robbiae*
☽ ● ↕ 30 ✿ 3-5

Syn. *E. robbiae*. Spreads widely by rhizomes and, eventually, develops into a broad plant. Rosettes of evergreen leaves and yellow-green flowers. Grows on the poorest soils but freezes in a severe winter.

E. corallioides
☼ ☽ ↕ 60 ✿ 6-8

Densely leaved stems bear long, fresh green leaves with clear, white central veins. Has widely branched umbels of yellow-green flowers throughout the summer. Short-lived but self-seeds well.

E. cyparissias 'Fens Ruby'
☼ ↕ 20 ✿ 4-6

A strongly rampant species with needlelike leaves and small yellow umbels. Useful because the plant emerges in spring in a pretty shade of purple and also because it will thrive in the driest spots. Lovely autumn color.

E. griffithii 'Dixter'
☼ ↕ 80 ✿ 5-6

A spectacular plant with bright orange inflorescences above lance-shaped red leaves. 'Dixter' grows more compactly than the common form, which is very invasive. Damp soil is a must for this plant.

E. palustris
☼ ☽ ↕ 120 ✿ 4-5

Marsh spurge is a tall, robust plant with large spring-flowering, pale-yellow clusters that continue to grow and flower well, given ordinary, moisture-retentive soil. In autumn the stems turn red and the leaves orange-yellow.

E. sarawschanica
☼ ☽ ↕ 120 ✿ 6-7

Narrow leaves and small ochre yellow clusters of flowers that tend to flop, not in an untidy way, but as a pleasant, noncommittal mound of green.

E. schillingii
☼ ☽ ↕ 120 ✿ 6-9

A tall, robust species bearing narrow, olive green leaves with white central veins and yellow green inflorescences that keep on flowering, endlessly.

Filipendula, Rosaceae, *meadow sweet*

Plants with magnificent pinnate leaves, of which those at the top are far larger than the lower ones. Produces masses of flowers in frothy, irregularly shaped racemes. All the species require fertile, humus-rich soil that must never be allowed to dry out.

F. kamtschatica
☼ ☽ ↕ 250 ✿ 6-7

A gigantic species with large cream-colored plumes. Suitable for a wild corner of the garden.

F. purpurea
☼ ☽ ↕ 80 ✿ 7-8

Airy plumes that appear to be floating on the stems. The color is a harsh shade of pink.
'Alba'
White flowers and light green stems.
'Elegans'
Flowers a softer shade of pink than the species.
'Nephele'
Taller (120 cm) than the species. The pink plumes fade to a paler shade.

F. rubra 'Venusta'
☼ ☽ ↕ 180 ✿ 7-8

The queen of the prairie, as the plant is called in North America, is a veritable giant with bright pink clusters of flowers that turn chestnut brown. The branches droop under the weight of the flower clusters but recover after the flowers die off. The plant remains attractive throughout winter.

Foeniculum, Apiaceae, *fennel*

F. vulgare
☼ ↕ 160 ✿ 7-9

One of the many soft-yellow flowering umbellifers that are so familiar in the southern European landscape. The needlelike, finely divided foliage and the herby smell of fennel add to this southern character. Another "southern" aspect of this plant is the fact that it does not tolerate severe winters. It does, however, seed itself freely. Grows on all types of soil but is at its best (and most aromatic) in arid, dry places.
'Giant Bronze'
Bronze-colored foliage. The most attractive form for the garden.

Galega, Fabaceae, *goat's rue*

Vetchlike plants with pinnate leaves and long sprays of papilionaceous flowers. *Galega officinalis*, well-known for ages, is hardly less than a disaster; it will not grow at all in some situations, in others it becomes an indestructible weed. A far superior species is *G. orientalis*.

G. orientalis
☼ ↕ 120 ✿ 5-7

This plant, with its elongated, clear blue racemes of flowers, looks very much like a giant vetch. It is slightly invasive because of its underground runners, but the flowers are sterile, so it does not seed itself, and it flowers over a long period.

Gaura, Onagraceae, *gaura*

G. lindheimeri
☼ ↕ 100 ✿ 7-10

A glorious plant with lax growth and long stems bearing many white flowers that look exactly like butterflies. Remains in flower until the first night frost. Unfortunately, the plant is short-lived and, therefore, more suitable for a first-year border or for filling up gaps in established borders.
'Siskiyou Pink'
Flowers pink.
'Whirling Butterflies'
Sturdier than the species and flowers even more profusely than the species.

Above left
The young foliage of
Epimedium grandiflorum 'Lilac Seedling'

Left
*Eryngium
xtripartitum*; with
Helenium
'Rubinzwerg' behind

Above
Filipendula rubra
'Venusta'

Above right
A pale blue seedling
of *Gentiana asclepiadea*

Right
Eupatorium maculatum 'Atropurpureum'
behind a bamboo and
Selinum wallichianum

Gentiana, Gentianaceae, *gentian*

A well-known genus of primarily high-mountain plants, the bell-shaped flowers of which are an eponymous gentian blue. Most of the species are for true garden enthusiasts; they are difficult to grow and flower poorly in low-lying areas. A few important exceptions are described here.

G. asclepiadea

☼ ◑ ↕ 60 ✿ 8-9

In the wild the willow gentian appears in fertile woods and beside streams in the chalk mountains of central European. Slightly arched stems, with willowlike leaves, bear many so-called gentian blue flowers over almost their complete length. When the plants feel at home (on moisture-retentive chalky soil) they can hold their own among indigenous vegetation.

'Alba'
Greenish-white flowers.

G. lutea

☼ ↕ 100 ✿ 6

The familiar yellow gentian, which cannot be overlooked as a feature of all western and southern European alpine meadows, will also grow on lower ground if it is good, well-drained, and not too fertile. Slow-growing plants with strong stems and large deeply veined, ovate, opposite leaves. The yellow flowers appear as small wreaths at the top of the stems and are followed by equally attractive seeds. The flowering demands so much energy that a plant often fails to flower the following year.

Geranium, Geraniaceae, *cranesbill*

Easy plants with attractive, round leaves that can be lobed or deeply palmate, attractive "proper" flowers (five petals, as they should), and an unusual smell. The species owes it English name to the fruits of the plant that show an amazing similarity to a crane's bill. Many hundreds of species and cultivars are grown and they are all attractive—so attractive that many genuine clubs have been set up by people who specialize in growing the *Geranium* species, to the exclusion of all other plants. Without attempting to be complete (an impossible task) we shall bring you up to date.

G. xcantabrigiense

☼ ◑ ↕ 25 ✿ 6-7

A cross between *G. dalmaticum* and *G. macrorrhizum* that is found in the wild. It is slightly invasive but not as vigorous as the latter species. A nice plant for ground cover.

'Biokovo'
White flowers on red stems.

'Cambridge'
Faster growing, with pinkish-red flowers.

G. clarkei **'Kashmir White'**

☼ ◑ ↕ 40 ✿ 5-7

Delicate, deeply cut foliage and a sea of lilac-veined white flowers. A delightful species but rather invasive. **'Kashmir Pink'** has candy pink flowers and **'Kashmir Purple'**, dark purple.

G. macrorrhizum

☼ ◑ ● ↕ 35 ✿ 5-6

A robust ground cover with pretty foliage and a strong smell. The pink flowers are encased in dark red bracts. Very strong, will thrive anywhere. The leaves remain on the plant in winter, when they turn orange-red.

'Album'
Flowers white.

'Czakor'
Grows taller than the species and bears magenta pink flowers.

G. maculatum

☼ ◑ ↕ 50 ✿ 4-6

An early flowering American species with deeply cut leaves and large pale lilac flowers on long stems. One of the prettiest species—the whole plant radiates grace.

G. nodosum

◑ ● ↕ 35 ✿ 5-10

An unassuming species with shiny, dark green leaves and lilac-blue flowers. Special for two reasons: the plant keeps on flowering, and it does so in the most impossible places, even at the foot of birch trees. But, be warned: give plenty of thought to where you would like it to grow because, once planted, it cannot be gotten rid of.

'Whiteleaf'
Does not have white leaves, as the name suggests, but white-edged dark purple-red flowers. Not as robust as the species.

G. xoxonianum

A generic term for a large number of hybrids from *G. endressii* and *G. versicolor*. A selection of cultivars follows.

'Rebecca Moss'
☼ ◑ ↕ 30 ✿ 6-9
Silvery pink flowers.

'Rose Clair'

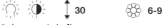

☼ ◑ ↕ 30 ✿ 6-9
The flowers turn from pinkish red to light pink.

'Sherwood'
Looks like 'Rose Clair' but the flowers are pale pink.

'Thurstonianum'
☼ ◑ ↕ 50 ✿ 6-9
A healthy grower with curious flowers: the pinkish-red petals are very narrow, just like little worms.

'Wageningen'
☼ ◑ ↕ 30 ✿ 6-9
Salmon-pink flowers.

G. palustre

☼ ↕ 40 ✿ 5-6

Unusual about this species, with its fairly ordinary, slightly scalloped pink-red petals, is that it also thrives in marshy places. Suitable for running wild near a pond.

G. phaeum

◑ ● ↕ 60-90 ✿ 5-7

The familiar dark cranesbill, or mourning widow, with its drooping, dark purple flowers on long stems. The plant is a prolific seeder and can easily hold its own in a wild garden. There are numerous cultivars, the most important of which are named here.

'Album'
Lighter green leaves and white, slightly more upward-pointing, shiny flowers.

'Calligrapher'
Flowers gray-white with a purple ring on the petals.

'Lily Lovell'
A large plant with violet-blue flowers.

'Rose Madder'
A slow grower with reddish-brown flowers touched with pink.

'Samobor'
Striking black marks on the leaves.

'Springtime'
Pretty, yellow variegated leaves which accentuate the flowers. Autumn coloring with orange and red in the foliage.

G. pratense

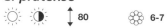

☼ ◑ ↕ 80 ✿ 6-7

The common species with blue flowers is inclined to collapse and is, therefore, only suitable for planting between tall grasses in a flowering meadow. This also applies to the cultivars 'Mrs. Kendall Clark', with veined flowers, and 'Silver Queen', with pale blue flowers and eye-catching black stamens.

'Victor Reiter'

☼ ◑ ↕ 40 ✿ 6

Reddish-brown leaves and dark blue flowers. Does not collapse.

'White Lady'

☼ ◑ ↕ 60 ✿ 6-7

Flowers white. Does not collapse.

G. psilostemon

☼ ◑ ↕ 80 ✿ 6-8

Syn. *G. armenum*. A strong, large species from Armenia that bears deep magenta flowers with black centers. Overwhelmingly beautiful. Seeds modestly and, in spite of its conspicuous color, fits in well with all plants.

G. renardii

☼ ↕ 35 ✿ 6-7

Magnificent white woolly, lobed foliage is the main decorative attraction of this plant. Not that the purple-veined white flowers are not pretty—they are sublime—but, unfortunately, they are short-lived. The foliage remains on the plant in mild winters.

'Philippe Vapelle'
Grows larger than the ordinary species and blooms more profusely. Flowers purple-blue.

G. sanguineum

☼ ↕ 25-50 ✿ 6-9

The bloody cranesbill is an extremely strong plant, as long as it has a place in the sun. It then blooms throughout the summer with vivid, pinkish-red flowers.

'Album'
Flowers chalky-white. A tall plant.
'Ankum's Pride'
Warm pink flowers with ribbed edges. Reaches 25 cm in height.
'Khan'
Very tall growing (50 cm) with magenta flowers.

G. sanguineum var. striatum

☼ ↕ 20 ✿ 6-8

Has light pink flowers with dark pink veins.

G. soboliferum

☼ ↕ 50 ✿ 7-9

A low, compact species with lilac-pink flowers throughout the summer. The autumn color is wonderful: yellow and reddish-orange.

G. sylvaticum 'Amy Doncaster'

☼ ◑ ↕ 60 ✿ 5-7

An easy-to-grow species, with shallowly lobed leaves and not very large deep blue flowers with white centers

G. wallichianum 'Buxton's Variety'

☼ ↕ 35 ✿ 7-11

A plant that spreads out and must be given an opportunity to clamber up between other plants. The lilac-blue, white-eyed flowers appear from July onwards. In autumn the plant flowers even more prolifically, while the foliage gradually turns orange-red.

G. wlassovianum

☼ ◑ ↕ 35 ✿ 7-9

Exceptional are the orange-pink leaves that emerge in spring and the lilac-colored flowers that appear late (for a G*eranium*, that is).

Geranium hybrids

G. 'Ann Folkard'

☼ ◑ ↕ 35 ✿ 6-9

Appears in spring with golden-yellow leaves and has purple flowers with black centers, borne on lax stems, which can eventually reach a meter in height. Long flowering. Suitable for planting between early flowering plants that are uninteresting later in the season. A good distracter.

G. 'Brookside'

☼ ◑ ↕ 60 ✿ 6-7

A sturdy plant, an improved version of the old 'Johnson's Blue', which has large almost true blue flowers. Flowers over a long period.

G. 'Dilys'

☼ ◑ ↕ 30 ✿ 7-11

Does not really get going until late summer, when it covers a large area. Handy for planting alongside plants that finish flowering early in the season (for example, *Papaver orientale*). The flowers are red-purple.

G. 'Sirak'

☼ ◑ ↕ 50 ✿ 6-7

Found in the wild in the Caucasus. Large lilac-pink flowers are so tightly veined that they seem to radiate light.

G. 'Spinners'

☼ ◑ ↕ 80 ✿ 8-9

A robust plant with large dark purple-blue flowers.

Geum, Rosaceae, *avens*

G. rivale

◑ ● ↕ 30 ✿ 4-0

The nodding avens is a subtle plant for shady places. It has pinnate leaves with a large rounded, terminal leaf and clusters of hanging flowers in spring. The flowers are brown with beige veins. Although the plant grows in the wild mainly close to streams and springs, it is an exceptionally easy garden plant. It even tends to be invasive. With a bit of luck it flowers for a second time in autumn.

'Beech House Apricot'
Apricot-colored flowers.
'Leonard'
Pink flowers, enclosed by velvety brown bracts.

Gillenia, Rosaceae

G. trifoliata

☼ ◑ ↕ 100 ✿ 6-7

Although this plant has been cultivated for a long time, it is still not widely known. We shall once again put in a good word for these sturdy plants with their long-flowering clouds of white flowers with red bracts on red flower stems. Although every book states that the plant requires moisture-retentive soil, our experience is that it grows well in a dry, semishady spot. Between us, the plant will grow almost anywhere.

Glaucium, Papaveraceae, *horned poppy*

G. corniculatum

☼ ↕ 60 ✿ 6-9

The red horned poppy is a biennial. During the first year, silver-gray rosettes of indented leaves are formed. In the second year, gray stems arise from the rosettes, bearing gray leaves, gray flower buds, and brilliant orange-red poppy flowers. Only a few flowers are open at the same time–throughout the whole summer–so that the

Top
Geranium nodosum
'Whiteleaf'

Above
*Geranium xoxoni-
anum* 'Thurstonianum'

Centre left
Geranium sylvaticum
'Amy Doncaster'

Left
Geranium psilostemon

Top
Gillenia trifoliata

Right
Geum rivale 'Leonard'

Above
Geranium phaeum

Left
Helenium 'Rubinkuppel'

Center far left
Helenium 'Kupferzwerg'

Below far left
Glycyrrhiza yunnanensis

Center left
Helianthus salicifolius

Below left
Helleborus odorus

Right
Heuchera micrantha 'Palace Purple'

Below
Hemerocallis 'Princess Blue Eyes'

Bottom
Hemerocallis 'Nugget'

'Frances Williams'
A wide, soft yellow-green margin around the blue-green leaf.

H. xtardiana

◐ ↕ 40   ✳ 7-8

Small leaved.
'Blue Moon'
The smallest of the *tardiana* hybrids, with wide, blue-gray leaves that end in sharp points. The flowers are light lilac.
'Halcyon'
Resembles a small *H. sieboldiana* 'Elegans', without the pronounced veins. The leaves are grayer than gray and overlap each other most elegantly. The flowers are lilac colored.

H. tokudama 'Hadspen Blue'

◐ ↕ 40   ✳ 7-8

Syn. *H. sieboldiana* var. *fortunei* 'Hadspen Blue'. Small, thick, gray-green foliage and lavender-blue flowers.

H. ventricosa 'Aureomarginata'

◐ ↕ 70   ✳ 7-8

Large ribbed leaves with a wide yellow-white margin. The violet-blue flowers on long stems are conspicuous.

Hosta hybrids and cultivars

'Blue Angel'

◐ ↕ 100   ✳ 7-8

Excessively large blue foliage and a noticeably compact inflorescence with white flowers, flushed lilac. Flowers over a very long period.
'Blue Impression'

◐ ↕ 45   ✳ 7-8

A medium-sized plant with blue-gray foliage and many lilac-colored flowers, which under a clouded sky seem to be blue.
'Krossa Regal'

◐ ↕ 100   ✳ 7-8

An absolute giant with narrow blue-gray leaves that point arrowlike upwards and lilac-colored flowers on noticeably long stems. This plant needs plenty of space.
'Midas Touch'

◐ ↕ 60   ✳ 7-8

Golden-yellow, round, deeply puckered, cupped leaves that look as if King Midas had touched them. You, too, may find it difficult to keep

your hands off them. The lilac inflorescences barely emerge above the foliage and are a very poor color match with the leaves, so it is better to remove them.
'Sum and Substance'

◐ ↕ 120   ✳ 7-8

Enormous, fresh green foliage which is so thick that the snails do not even attempt to eat it.
'White Triumphator'

◐ ↕ 120   ✳ 7-8

A hosta whose flowers are the most important part of the plant: they are large and white and grow on long stems.

Houttuynia, Saururaceae

H. cordata

 ↕ 30   ✳ 7-8

An extremely rampant, ground-covering plant with wonderful, slanting, heart-shaped foliage that is red-brown when it emerges through the soil. The foliage sticks to this color in sunshine but reverts to dark green in the shade. Small creamy white flowers with tall green seed cones. Thrives only on damp soil but can then overrun everything in a jiffy. Be warned!

Inula, Asteraceae, *fleabane*

A large genus of plants with ordinary foliage and just as ordinary yellow daisylike flowers. So nothing special, apart from the fact that a few species stand out.

I. hookeri

☀ ◐ ↕ 60   ✳ 8-10

A lanky plant covered in thick foliage. Spreads considerably. The plentiful narrow, bright yellow ray florets wriggle in a curious fashion out of the attractive, hairy involucral bracts.

I. magnifica

☀ ↕ 220   ✳ 7-8

A giant plant with big flaps of leaves and sturdy stems, branched at the top, which bear enormous yellow daisylike flowers with many narrow ray florets.
'Sonnenstrahl'
Found on a compost heap by German nurseryman Ernst Pagels. The ray flowers are so long that they hang over attractively.

Iris, Iridaceae, *Iris*

A familiar genus of plants with many hundreds of species. The flowering period is very short but so exceptional that the plants are grown on a large scale. We shall not take the trouble to describe them, because to do them justice would take a whole page of print. Moreover, everyone knows what they look like. The characteristic, swordlike leaves remain beautiful throughout the summer.

I. chrysographes

☀ ↕ 70   ✳ 6

A very uncommon iris with eccentric, velvety black and bluish-purple flowers. The plant definitely requires moisture-retentive soil.

I. foetidissima

☀ ↕ 60   ✳ 6-7

A winter-green species which, contrary to the other irises, enjoys growing in shade. The plant has an unusual smell of roast meat and is, therefore, sometimes called the roast beef plant in England. The flowers are an unpretentious shade of lilac, but when the large seed heads open in the autumn, they turn out to be full of bright orange seeds—quite a spectacle in the autumn garden.

Kalimeris, Asteraceae

Sturdy, shrublike perennials that form round hillocks covered with large (3 cm across) daisies. They are the kind of plants you pass by indifferently, thinking, "Oh, just another aster," until you realize that they are flowering rather early for asters, which they are not although they have a truly lovely shape. So on second thought, they are perfect border plants that fit in everywhere; you just cannot have enough of them.

K. incisa

☀ ↕ 90   ✳ 6-9

Known as cast-iron plant. Regularly shaped and flowering all summer long with numerous lilac-blue daisy flowers.
'Alba'
Similar to the species but with white flowers.

K. pinnatifida 'Hortensis'

☀ ↕ 100   ✳ 9-10

An autumn-flowering plant with indented leaves and semidouble flowers with yellow centers.

Kirengeshoma, Hydrangeaceae, *Japanese waxflower*

K. palmata
◑ ● ↕ 100 ✿ 9-10

Shade plants with wonderful, corrugated, sycamore-like leaves. The appearance of the leaves in spring is quite an occasion: fat leaf buds, with lovely patterned dentate edges slowly unfold. In summer soft yellow buds are formed, which grow very slowly until, in late summer, the large waxlike bellflowers open. Afterwards, the seed capsules, adorned with three needles, remain attractive for a long period. Kirengeshomas grow and flower almost everywhere, as long as the soil does not dry out. They are one of the few plants that flower in places where the sun never shines.

Koreana group
Flowers open slightly better than those of the species and they are horizontal.

Knautia, Dipsacaceae

At first sight *Knautia* and *Scabiosa* are as alike as two drops of water. The difference is technical—something to do with the one having strawlike scales, the other not. This can only be seen (with a magnifying glass) after the flower has been dissected. Moreover, *Knautia* species are generally more robust than *Scabiosa* species. Butterflies could not care less: they love them both.

K. dipsacifolia
☼ ◑ ↕ 120 ✿ 6-8

A large well-branched plant that collapses easily and has rather coarse foliage but which is laden from top to bottom with purple flowers. A real treat for insects. It is at its best in a wilder part of the garden, between shrubs and tall grass.

K. drymeia
☼ ◑ ↕ 50 ✿ 6-8

Resembles *K. dipsacifolia*, but is much shorter and has lilac-pink flowers.

K. macedonica
☼ ↕ 60 ✿ 7-9

Bears magnificent, claret-colored flowers throughout the summer and tends to set seed, but this is no problem because you can never have too many of these plants.

Lamium, Lamiaceae, *dead nettle*

Dead nettles are very familiar with their large whorls of lipped flowers and their uninhibited rampant growth. There are also noninvasive species.

L. maculatum
☼ ◑ ↕ 15 ✿ 4-9

The common lilac-pink-flowered species is extremely rampant. The two cultivars described here are not.
'Pink Pewter'
White, sharply toothed leaves with green margins. Flowers shrimp pink.
'White Nancy'
Silvery white leaves and white flowers.

L. orvala
◑ ● ↕ 50 ✿ 4-5

A dead nettle species from central Europe that does not develop runners and is absolutely noninvasive. The dark green wrinkled foliage appears in early spring, the underside is then purple-red. This plant has larger flowers than the other dead nettles, and they are light brownish pink with darker spots or stripes.
'Album'
A form with dingy white flowers and light green leaves.

Lavatera, Malvaceae

Closely related to mallow (*Malva*), from which it is hardly distinguishable, even by specialized botanists. *Lavatera* often has a shrublike character and, in general, is more ornamental. Typical palmately lobed leaves and five-petaled flowers with scalloped petals. The stamens grow into tufts. The most well-known species, the woody based **L. olbia**, and the related cultivars **'Barnsley'** and **'Burgundy Wine'** are not hardy and have, moreover, the awful habit of forming different, and generally uglier-colored, off-shoots.

L. cachemiriana
☼ ↕ 160 ✿ 7-9

A perennial that dies back to ground level in winter. The flowers, which keep appearing on the plants for a long period, are silky pink and have noticeably narrow petals, so that the light green sepals remain clearly visible. An exceptionally beautiful species that is hardy.
'White Angel'
Satin white flowers.

L. cachemiriana x L. thuringiaca
☼ ↕ 160 ✿ 7-9

The following hybrids have overlapping petals and are fully to reasonably hardy.
'Summer Kisses'
Deep pink flowers and only 140 cm tall.
'Sweet Dream'
Pink flowers.
'White Satin'
Double, white flowers.

Leucanthemella, Asteraceae, *marguerite*

L. serotina
☼ ↕ 160 ✿ 9-10

Syn. *Chrysanthemum serotinum*. A tall autumn-flowering marguerite with a green center. Because the flowers always turn to face the sun, be careful where you plant them; otherwise you could be looking at the back of the flowers.

Liatris, Asteraceae

Familiar, stiff-looking plants with narrow, grassy leaves and truncheon-shaped inflorescences. The reddish-purple thistlelike flowers open from the top to the bottom of the stem. They are very popular as cut flowers, but there has never been a demand for them as garden plants. However, planted among ornamental grasses they lose all their stiffness. They thrive best in fertile, moisture-retentive garden soil.

L. aspera
☼ ↕ 100 ✿ 7-8

The most ornamental species. The flower heads are not crammed together but spread along the stem, and the spikes are wider at the bottom.

L. ligulistylis
☼ ↕ 100 ✿ 7-8

A slender plant with upward-pointing flower heads that in bud look like miniature red cabbages.

L. pycnostachya
☼ ↕ 120 ✿ 7-8

A tall species that strongly resembles *L. spicata*, but it has longer inflorescences so that the whole plant seems more slender.

Left
Hosta xtardiana 'Halcyon'

Below far left
Lavatera cachemiriana x *L. thuringiaca*
'White Satin'

Below left
Knautia macedonica in front of *Eryngium giganteum* and *Glaucium corniculatum*

Right
Liatris ligulistylis

Below
Lamium orvala 'Album'

'Beau
Bright
'Flam
A stu
flowe
gins.
'Julia
A tal
petti
'Kar
Flat,
the
'Kle
Rem
strik
the
'Lila
Of
ers.
wa
'Pe
An
bla
'Pi
A
wh
of

P

A
le
sp
in
H
s
i
w
p
s

Left
Limonium latifolium with
the small flowers of *Dianthus
carthusianorum*

Below far left
Lindelofia anchusoides

Centre left
Linaria purpurea 'Springside
White' with *Monarda* 'Snow
Queen'

Below left
Lobelia 'Eulalia Berridge'

Right
Mertensia virginica

Below
Lychnis chalcedonica 'Alba'

Below right
Lythrum salicaria 'Blush'

Bottom
Lysimachia ephemerum and
Echinacea paradoxa between
Amsonia hubrichtii, *Panicum
virgatum* 'Cloud Nine' (left) and
P. virgatum 'Rehbraun'

With
is a v
'Gar
Flow
culti
dam
cult
'Mc
A ta
ers
'Ou
A s
ab
'Pa
A
gr
'S
A
e
'S
w
"
A
is

!

Left
Monarda 'Pawnee'

Center left
Nepeta govaniana

Below
Origanum vulgare
'Herrenhausen' between
Perovskia abrotanoides 'Blue
Spire' and *Achillea*
'Wesersandstein'

Bottom
Papaver orientale 'Karine'

Right
Persicaria amlexicaulis 'Firedance'
behind *Phlox paniculata*
'Düsterlohe'

Below right
Petalostemum purpureum

Centre far right
Persicaria polymorpha

Below far right
Persicaria bistorta subsp. *carnea*

Left
Phlox paniculata 'Lichtspel'. On the right
Veronicastrum virginicum 'Roseum' and
Lavatera cachemiriana

Center far left
Phlox divaricata 'May Breeze'

Below far left
Phlox paniculata

Below left
Platycodon grandiflorus 'Perlmutterschale'

Right
Phlomis tuberosa 'Amazone' in front of
Crambe cordifolia

Below
Phlomis taurica

Bottom
Pimpinella major var. *rosea*

Below right
Polygonatum xhybridum
'Weihenstephan'

Top
Potentilla *thurberi*

Center left
A *Pulmonaria* hybrid
leaf

Left
Rodgersia pinnata 'Die
Anmutige' between
Melica nutans

Above
Salvia nemorosa
'Pink Delight'

Above right
Salvia nemorosa
'Serenade'

Above far right
Salvia azurea

Right
Salvia verticillata
'Purple Rain'

Far right
Salvia glutinosa

Above left
Scutellaria incana

Left
Sedum telephium
subsp. *maximum*
'Atropurpureum'

Top
Sanguisorba officinalis
'Red Thunder'

Above
Selinum wallichianum

Above right
Sanguisorba menziesii

Center right
Serratula seoanei

Right
Sidalcea oregana
'Little Princess'

Far right
Silphium laciniatum

Above left
Solidago rugosa

Center left
Solidago
'Goldenmosa'

Below left
Succisa pratensis

Left
Stachys officinalis
'Rosea'

Top
Thalictrum delavayi
with *Phlox paniculata*

Above
Thalictrum polygamum

Right
Thalictrum 'Elin'

Planting the Natural Garden

Above left
Tricyrtis 'Shimone'

Far left
Valeriana pyrenaica

Left
Trifolium pannonicum

Top
Verbascum lychnitis
with *Campanula
lactiflora*

Above
Trifolium rubens, to
the left *Teucrium
hircanicum*

Right
Veratrum nigrum

flowers for a short time, but it is very special: whereas all violet-blues tend toward purple, this "tall violet" has almost sky-blue flowers with a white center eye. This is a little gem for a shaded garden. It prefers to seed itself between gravel and stones.

V. labradorica

◑ ● ↕ 5 ✿ 4

By far the most important garden plant among the wood violets. Its flowering season is just as short as that of the other species, but the attractive, purple-hued foliage is present the whole year. The plant spreads by rhizomes and seeds in splits and holes; it is the ideal gap filler in shade gardens.

V. sororia

◑ ● ↕ 10 ✿ 4-5

A violet that forms large clumps and, moreover, seeds itself freely, so it is very suitable as ground cover in a wild garden.
'Albiflora'
Flowers white.
'Freckles'
White flowers with purple spots. A little darling.

Zigadenus, Melanthiaceae

Z. elegans subsp. glaucus

☼ ◑ ↕ 60 ✿ 7-8

A slow-growing but strong plant with stiff, bluish-green grassy leaves, gray-green stems, and beige-colored, green-speckled, starlike flowers. Subtle in every detail and delightful when combined with other plants.

Above left
Veronicastrum virginicum 'Roseum'

Left
Zigadenus elegans subsp. *glaucus*

Above
Viola sororia 'Freckles'

Right
Viola elatior

Ornamental Grasses

<u>Achnatherum</u>, Poaceae

A. calamagrostis

☼ ↕ 90　　❀ 6-9

Syn. *Stipa calamagrostis*. Forms a loose clump and gracefully arching, richly flowering panicles that are initially silver-colored but quickly turn to khaki. Remains effective until deep into the autumn.

<u>Asperella</u>, Poaceae, *bottlebrush grass*

A. hystrix

☼ ↕ 80　　❀ 6-7

Syn. *Hystrix patula*. From an untidy mophead of overhanging grass, narrow, lax bottlebrush-like spikes appear in summer. Very attractive but slow growing. Is best on humus-rich soil with good drainage.

<u>Brachypodium</u>, Poaceae, *slender false brome*

B. sylvaticum

☼ ◑ ● ↕ 80　　❀ 6-8

The false brome forms clumps of broad, light green, long hairy leaves. The compact spikelets that resemble small lockets are on graceful

spikes. The plant is effective for almost the whole year: when the flowering season is over the spikes remain until, in early spring, the fresh green clumps reappear. Tolerates deep shade and drought. An ideal ornamental grass, were it not for the fact that it spreads. Some gardening experience is desirable.

<u>Briza</u>, Poaceae, *quaking grass*

B. media

☼ ↕ 40　　❀ 5-7

A low-growing, tussock-forming grass, with blue-green foliage and graceful, loose flower plumes. The glossy green and purple spikelets dangle on threadlike, crooked stems and "quake" in the slightest puff of wind. A suitable species for dried-flower arrangements. A good plant for a sunny, not-too-dry, and certainly not-too-fertile spot.
'Limouzi'
A better choice for more fertile ground and taller growing (70 cm) than the species.

<u>Calamagrostis</u>, Poaceae, *small reed*

C. xacutiflora

☼ ↕ 180　　❀ 6-7

A natural hybrid of *C. epigejos,* dune reed, and

Hakonechloa macra (left) and *Deschampsia cespitosa.* Behind *Lythrum virgatum* (centre) and *Lavatera cachemiriana* (right)

C. arundinacea. Noninvasive. This sturdy, upright grass appears very early in the year and forms slender brown spikes on man-sized stems in summer. In summer the spikes bleach to a flaxen yellow color. Remains sturdy throughout the winter and, therefore, effective. Charming as a solitary grass or when combined with attractive shrubs.
'Karl Foerster'
Should there be storms and a lot of rainfall during the flowering season (June) the inflorescences easily snap off, but once it has finished flowering the plant is as steady as a house.
'Overdam'
Has white-variegated foliage and a purple flush to the stems and inflorescence. Is a slightly shorter (160 cm) form.

C. brachytricha

☼ ↕ 120　　❀ 8-10

A stunningly beautiful grass. From the rather nondescript clumps, extremely long, loose, rounded panicles emerge in late summer. During damp weather the panicle is covered with drops of water, so we call it diamond grass.

Carex, Cyperaceae, *sedge*

Sedges differ from ordinary grasses in that the flowers are always grouped together on spikes. Stems and leaves are usually sharp, three-sided, and dull green, yellow, or brownish. With the sedge species, the spikelets are generally on individual stems, scattered along the stalk. The male and female flowers are usually on separate spikes. Of the 2000 known sedge species, the greatest number of them grows on mean haylands, marshes, or mountain meadows. Cattle avoid the sharp-edged grasses, so the farmers do not like to see them in their fields. Luckily (for them), they do not tolerate manure or fertilizer, so that nowadays they are only found in the wild in nature reserves. Luckily (for us) there are species that thrive in gardens. They form wonderful clumps.

C. elata 'Aurea'

☼ ◑ ↕ 70   ✿ 4-5

Syn. *C. stricta* 'Aurea'. On moist soil or in shallow water this plant forms huge clumps, or horsts, that can easily bear the weight of a human being. A great marsh can be crossed by jumping from clump to clump. 'Aurea' is interesting for the garden with its yellow, green-margined foliage.

C. grayi

☼ ◑ ↕ 60   ✿ 5-10

The morningstar sedge is a large plant with rather broad leaves. After the inconspicuous flowers, large pointed seeds form, which are joined together into prickly seed heads. They look exactly like a mace, the weapon with which people in the Middle Ages attacked each other. The seeds remain on the plant until deep into the autumn. Remains green in mild winters and grows easily in almost all types of soil.

C. muskingumensis

☼ ◑ ↕ 60   ✿ 6-7

Looks exactly like papyrus with its narrow, arching leaves growing around the stem. An extremely graceful species for damp places.

C. pendula

◑ ↕ 150   ✿ 5-7

Pendulous sedge forms huge horsts that can be more than 1 m tall and wide. The flowers are distinctive with long, pendent spikelets on man-sized arching stems. They are found in the wild especially beside woodland streams and near springs. Also grows easily in the garden in semishade on drier soil.

Chasmantium, Poaceae, *sea oats*

C. latifolium

☼ ◑ ↕ 80   ✿ 9-10

Syn. *Uniola latifolia*. A stiff, erect plant with wide leaves and curiously flat, elliptical spikes. After flowering the blades of grass arch over.

Deschampsia, Poaceae, *hair grass*

D. cespitosa

☼ ◑ ↕ 120   ✿ 6-7

One of our most beautiful and common indigenous grasses, although hardly anyone will recognize it in the wild. It is barely noticeable between other grasses, where it prefers to grow on waterlogged soil. As a garden plant, hair grass forms large clumps of long, narrow, dark green leaves that remain so throughout the winter. The inflorescences, on long stems, are very delicate and remain attractive for a long period after flowering. Grows on most soils that are not too dry.
'Goldschleier'
Inflorescences and stalks turn flaxen early in summer and, therefore, attract more attention.
'Goldtau'
Resembles 'Goldschleier', but is in all aspects smaller and more compact and flowers a little later.

Diarrhena, Poaceae

D. japonica

◑ ● ↕ 50   ✿ 7-8

An attractive grass for shade, with luminous, bright green leaves and an open, transparent inflorescence.

Eragrostis, Poaceae, love grass

A large genus of about 300 species of grasses, with refined inflorescences. Occurs worldwide in mainly dry, tropical and subtropical areas. Surprisingly enough, many of the species are also hardy in colder regions, as long as they have a sunny spot to grow in.

E. curvula

☼ ↕ 70   ✿ 7-9

Forms large horsts of threadlike leaves and long, gracefully arching, flowering blades.

E. spectabilis

☼ ↕ 30   ✿ 7-11

Forms a clump-sized leaf, above which countless, short-stemmed, airily branched flower panicles conjure up a reddish-brown carpet of stars.

E. trichodes

☼ ↕ 100   ✿ 8-10

Forms a tall, very fragile, silver-pink cloud.

Festuca, Poaceae, *fescue*

F. mairei

☼ ↕ 80   ✿ 6-7

Within two years this plant forms a meter-wide tussock of pendulous, blue-green leaves and slightly arching inflorescences.

Hakonechloa, Poaceae

H. macra

☼ ◑ ↕ 40   ✿ 8-9

Forms delightful mopheads of long, arching leaves. Lax flower panicles. The foliage turns orange in autumn. Fertile, well-drained soil is essential.
'Aureola'
Has bronze, yellow-striped leaves.

Imperata, Poaceae, *Japanese bloodgrass*

☼ ↕ 30   ✿ n/a

I. cylindrica 'Red Baron'
A clump-forming grass with short rhizomes. From its appearance in spring until autumn it has blood-red foliage. It does not flower. Just the plant (in Japanese style) to use in large groups in a strictly architecturally designed garden.

Milium, Poaceae, *millet*

M. effusum 'Aureum'

◑ ● ↕ 60   ✿ 4-6

A grass that forms runners. In spring, it has bright yellow foliage and sparkling yellow, open inflorescences. According to G. S. Thomas, "the whole grace of spring time in color and quality." Later in the year the leaves turn yellowish green. A wonderful plant for highlighting dark corners.

Above left
Imperata cylindrica
'Red Baron'

Left
Miscanthus sinensis
'Silberturm'

Top
Chasmantium latifolium

Above
Eragrostis spectabilis

Above right
Miscanthus sinensis
'Morning Light'

Center right
Left *Miscanthus sinensis*
'Zwergelefant', and
behind *Panicum virgatum*
'Heavy Metal'

Right
Molinia caerulea
'Moorhexe'

Far right
Molinia caerulea var.
arundinacea 'Windsäule',
with *Aconitum carmichaelii*
var. *wilsonii* in front

Miscanthus, Poaceae, *silver grass*

M. sinensis

A large reed species with long, pendulous foliage. Forms large clumps from which, at the end of the summer, elegant, reddish-brown inflorescences appear. After flowering, they bleach to silver. An extraordinarily decorative grass that can often be seen on Chinese and Japanese wood carvings. In autumn, the foliage turns yellow and orange and in the winter the whole plant becomes parchment white. Throughout the winter, the old flowering stems weather storms, rain or snow, without breaking. Traditionally a poor or nonflowering species in Europe. However, many new forms have come onto the market lately, mostly from Ernst Pagels, a nurseryman in Leer, Germany, and they do flower.

'Ferner Osten'

☼ ↕ 180 ❀ 9-11

A graceful, slender plant with narrow foliage and horizontal spikes. Has a lovely autumn color.

'Flamingo'

☼ ↕ 180 ❀ 8-10

An elegant, slender plant with arching, silver pink inflorescences.

'Gewitterwolke'

☼ ↕ 200 ❀ 8-10

Loosely shaped, blonde flowering plumes, like the peaks of a thunder cloud.

'Ghana'

☼ ↕ 180 ❀ 8-10

A narrow, erect plant with early autumn coloring.

'Graziella'

☼ ↕ 175 ❀ 8-10

An upright-growing plant with a lax, silver-colored inflorescence.

'Haiku'

☼ ↕ 300 ❀ 8-10

A slender, very tall, erect plant with an airy, silvery blond inflorescence.

'Hermann Müssel'

☼ ↕ 200 ❀ 8-10

Forms a broad clump and has a golden inflorescence.

'Kaskade'

☼ ↕ 210 ❀ 9-11

Arching stems and a pink flowering inflorescence that turns to straw white.

'Kleine Fontäne'

☼ ↕ 180 ❀ 7-10

Silvery, reddish-brown inflorescences early in the season. Keeps on producing new flower stems until the autumn.

'Kleine Silberspinne'

☼ ↕ 160 ❀ 8-10

Grows like a pouffe: wide tussocks with shoe-string leaves and many, narrow plumes of silvery red flowers.

'Krater'

☼ ↕ 170 ❀ 9-10

Forms a wide, not too tall clump.

'Malepartus'

☼ ↕ 200 ❀ 8-10

The bract, which surrounds the inflorescence before flowering, is strongly ribbed. When the reddish-brown flowers open they have a "shivering" look about them, which lasts for some time. A wonderful cultivar.

'Morning Light'

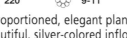
☼ ↕ 160 ❀ nvt

A delightful cultivar that does not flower or only sparsely so. Forms a large vase-shaped clump with gracefully arching, narrow, silver-veined leaves.

'Undine'

☼ ↕ 220 ❀ 9-11

A well-proportioned, elegant plant with strikingly beautiful, silver-colored inflorescences.

'Yakushima Dwarf'

☼ ↕ 120 ❀ 9-10

A small cultivar with narrow leaves and an open, reddish-silver inflorescence. Spreads by runners.

'Zwergelefant'

☼ ↕ 220 ❀ 8-10

The bract does not open at the top so that the reddish-silver flowering stems have to push themselves out from the bottom, still rolled-up. With a bit of imagination, they look like an elephant's trunk.

Molinia, Poaceae, *moor grass*

Although moor grass has had a bad reputation since its explosive growth at the expense of our heathland, which is a result of too much nitrogen in the air, it is and remains a regal plant. Especially in autumn, the heathlands and acid woods are crowned by the large clumps, as they turn orange-yellow. The flowering panicles are usually compressed into a narrow spike, sometimes they are loosely branched.

M. caerulea var. arundinacea

Syns. *M. altissima, M. litoralis*. Grows very tall with large loosely branched flower plumes. The plants turn golden yellow in autumn. Unfortunately, in winter they fall over.

'Cordoba'

☼ ◐ ↕ 220 ❀ 7-10

Arching flower stems that move elegantly in the wind, like a bullfighter.

'Fontäne'

☼ ◐ ↕ 180 ❀ 7-10

Dark, dense spikes on heavily arched stalks, suitable as a solitary grass between shorter plants.

'Karl Foerster'

☼ ◐ ↕ 220 ❀ 7-10

Stiffly erect with a brownish-yellow inflorescence.

'Transparent'

☼ ◐ ↕ 220 ❀ 7-10

Arching stalks and loose, pendent inflorescences.

'Windsäule'

☼ ◐ ↕ 250 ❀ 7-10

Tight, upright stalks that brave the elements (until the winter).

M. caerulea 'Edith Dudszus'

☼ ◐ ↕ 90 ❀ 7-10

A strong plant with compressed, dark inflorescences that are slightly arched.

M. caerulea 'Heidebraut'

☼ ◐ ↕ 120 ❀ 7-10

Fresh green with a loosely branched inflorescence. Brilliant autumn color.

M. caerulea 'Moorflamme'

☼ ◐ ↕ 70 ❀ 7-10

Turns flaming red in autumn.

M. caerulea 'Moorhexe'

☼ ◐ ↕ 70 ❀ 7-10

Characterized by numerous, stiffly erect, dark flowering spikes.

M. caerulea 'Poul Petersen'

☼ ◐ ↕ 60 ❀ 7-10

Very graceful, with its lightly arched flowering stalks and delightful orange-yellow autumn colors.

Panicum, Poaceae, *millet*

P. virgatum
A clump-forming grass that only starts to grow late in the season and flowers in summer like an ethereal, transparent cloud.

'Cloud Nine'
☼ ↕ 220 ✿ 8-10

A giant, with sturdy, gray-blue foliage and a vase-shaped growth.

'Dallas Blues'
☼ ↕ 160 ✿ 8-10

Broad, blue-gray leaves and an extra large silver-colored inflorescence.

'Heavy Metal'
☼ ↕ 120 ✿ 8-10

A stiff, blue-gray plant with an especially noticeable airy inflorescence.

'Rehbraun'
☼ ↕ 120 ✿ 8-10

An old cultivar whose foliage turns red-brown in summer.

'Shenandoah'
☼ ↕ 120 ✿ 8-10

The color change is more intense than with 'Rehbraun', but the plant grows slowly.

Pennisetum, Poaceae, *fountain grass*

P. alopecuroides
Clump-forming grasses with unusual, bottle-brush-shaped inflorescences at the end of summer.

'Cassian'
☼ ↕ 90 ✿ 8-11

Vase-shaped with arching, eye-catching dark spikes. Yellow autumn color.

'Woodside'
☼ ↕ 70 ✿ 8-11

A shorter form with narrow leaves and lightly arched inflorescences.

P. orientale
☼ ↕ 80 ✿ 8-10

A richly flowering species with straw-colored, long spikes that turn to silver. Needs a winter coat in severe winters.

P. viridescens
☼ ↕ 100 ✿ 9-10

Flowers later but has (in our climate) the darkest flowering plumes.

Schizachyrium, Poaceae

S. scoparium 'The Blues'
☼ ↕ 90 ✿ 6-7

One of the most important grasses from the North American prairie. Turns a wonderful reddish brown to orange in autumn.

Sesleria, Poaceae, *blue grass*

Low, clump-forming grasses with stiff, blue-green leaves that prefer to grow in the hottest and most arid spots on steep, limestone cliffs. We shall discuss two species that grow a little taller and thrive in ordinary garden soil.

S. autumnalis
☼ ◑ ↕ 40 ✿ 8-9

Forms clumps of bright green, almost transparent foliage that remains fresh-looking, and narrow, grayish-white spikelets that later turn brown.

S. nitida
☼ ↕ 60 ✿ 4-5

Forms hefty clumps that can become a meter in diameter. The narrow, gray-blue foliage has a metal sheen. Flowers early in the year with small oval, gray-white spikelets. Thrives on sandy, well-drained soil.

Sorghastrum, Poaceae, *golden beard grass*

S. nutans
☼ ↕ 160 ✿ 8-10

Syn. *Chrysopogon nutans*. One of the most important grasses of the tall grass prairie. Has arched stems and large brownish-purple flower panicles, which bear arresting, bright yellow anthers.

'Sioux Blue'
Steel-blue foliage.

Spodiopogon, Poaceae

S. sibiricus
☼ ◑ ↕ 120 ✿ 7-8

A bushy plant from the steppes of eastern Asia with sturdy blades and narrow flowering panicles. The plant has an aura of restraint about it. The color changes in summer from green to brown.

Sporobolus, Poaceae

S. heterolepis
☼ ↕ 80 ✿ 7-10

Forms elegant tussocks and lax, spike-shaped plumes filled with tiny pearls, which give off a sweet smell on warm days. Orange-yellow autumn coloring.

Stipa, Poaceae, *feather grass*

A large genus of steppe grasses with threadlike leaves and slender, graceful inflorescences. Each flower has a conspicuous, needle-shaped extension (the awn). All the species desire a dry, well-drained soil. At their best during warm summers. Easily disappear after a wet winter but seed well. The seedlings are easily distinguishable from other (weed) grasses by their threadlike foliage.

S. barbata
☼ ↕ 60 ✿ 6-7

Regularly shaped, slightly arching plumes, with long, pale green awns, appearing above dull green foliage.

S. gigantea
☼ ↕ 225 ✿ 6-8

Densely tufted clumps of grass with huge, oat-like inflorescences on long stems.

S. pulcherrima
☼ ↕ 100 ✿ 5-7

Syn. *S. pennata* subsp. *mediterranea*. Gray foliage and long (at least 50 cm) whiplike awns that start to flutter in a strong wind.

S. turkestanica
☼ ↕ 80 ✿ 7-8

Sea-green foliage and blond-flowering plumes. The awns are slightly spiral shaped. A strong species.

Above left
Stipa pulcherrima

Left
Sesleria nitida

Top
Pennisetum viridescens

Above
Sesleria autumnalis

Above right
Panicum virgatum
'Dallas Blues'

Center right
Panicum virgatum
'Rehbraun'

Right
Sporobolus heterolepis

Far right
Sorghastrum nutans

Uses

There are a thousand and one uses for the "Dream Plants" described and many more, too. To help you get started we offer a few suggestions. You can adopt them for your own garden: completely or partially, or become inspired when realizing your own plans, or cast them aside with a shudder of revulsion as examples of what not to do.

The main border in the Priona gardens with, among others, two giant examples of *Persicaria polymorpha*

In our nursery and gardens we are very aware of the infinite ways in which plants can be combined. Even our gardens are far too small to demonstrate them all, so we have decided to base our examples on a number of restrictive factors.

First, you can consider the *ecological* situation as a restrictive factor. This is logical, for you cannot grow sunflowers in a garden that has only one hour of sunlight a day, and when you have to wade through mud up to your ankles you will not consider growing succulents. From the dozens of examples that come to mind when considering the *ecological* situation of a garen, we have chosen two: *Blazing*–plants and possibilities for a hot, arid and dry garden in full sunlight, and *Lush*–plants and possibilities for a cool garden with fertile, moisture-retentive soil in semi-shade.

Another restrictive factor is the *architecture* of the garden: the shape and layout of the garden itself, the type of garden boundaries and the shape of neighboring gardens. Where gardens are small, the surrounding areas become relatively more important. Are there conspicuous architectural elements (such as buildings, or eye-catching plants and large trees) in the surrounding area, or is there nothing of note? Are there conspicuous architectural elements that, in your opinion, are not worthy of the name, such as a dilapidated shed or a wattle fence hand-made by the neighbor and not quite up to standard! The plants in your garden can either hide from view such undesirable architectural elements or act as a foil for the more desirable elements, for the plants themselves determine to a greater or lesser extent the *architecture*. An apparently unimportant group of plants that can add surprisingly to the architecture of a garden is described in the chapter titled *Airy*.

Having said all this you will be thinking? "And what about me and my garden?" Exactly. Now that your garden is both ecologically and architecturally sound you may voice your opinion. You are the one who has to look at the garden, day in, day out. You may be more interested in the *atmosphere* of the garden than in its color and form. When you look outside do you wish to become tranquil, happy or inspired? It is, therefore, important to consider the atmosphere that the plants radiate. Even more important is the atmosphere that a group of plants radiates. This can be subtle, wild, sophisticated or rather wooden—to mention only a few. Every assessment of a garden is, in fact, an assessment of atmosphere. "Beautiful" or "ugly" do not suffice. Only by mentioning the atmosphere (or the lack of it) do you say something essential about a garden.

The chapters *Tranquillity* and *Exuberant* have been written with this concept in mind.

The shape and/or color of a garden Is one of the most Important restrictive factors. For most gardeners this is by far the easiest method of garden design, because it is based on simple principles that are apparent to everyone. It is possibly the best way for beginners to learn about gardening. At a later stage the art can be refined by integrating more colors or one of the other restrictive factors. That gardening in color is not only intended for beginners will be apparent by the large number of sublime gardens that are open to the public, both at home and abroad. (One can hardly designate Vita Sackville West a beginner!) The chapter *Silvery* presents an example of gardening in color and the chapter titled *Grassy* gives examples of gardening with shape as the most important principle.

One of the restrictions that many gardeners voluntarily impose upon themselves is determined by their own impatience. In spring they dash outside and search all the markets and nurseries for attractive flowering plants. The result is that for such gardeners the height of the flowering season is reached in May and June. Afterwards, the garden gradually deteriorates, only to be relieved by the flowering of phlox at the end of July and the obligatory tuft of asters in October. This is obviously not the right approach. After all, we are happy to see a single flower in May—a garden full of flowering perennials is out of place. In spring we are more than satisfied with the fresh sprouting green (and possibly the flowers) of shrubs and the profusely flowering bulbs. Only in May and June are flowering perennials allowed to come into their own so that they reach their zenith at the height of summer (at the end of July or beginning of August). Then the garden can be allowed to gradually slow down until the last perennials finally finish flowering in November. The chapter titled *Autumn* describes all those perennials that commence flowering after midsummer.

Even after autumn the garden can remain attractive. Many perennials and ornamental grasses have beautiful winter silhouettes that keep the garden interesting until the following spring, and not only when the sun is low on the horizon or during periods of frost or snow. You will find these plants and grasses in the chapter titled *Gloomy*?

We shall conclude this introductory chapter on Uses with a few of our unbridled thoughts. Dreamlike combinations that keep us awake at night. Just imagine a massive planting of *Carex pendula* interspersed with a huge number of *Persicaria*

amplexicaulis 'Firedance' and a few robust heads of *Filipendula rubra* 'Venusta Magnifica' towering above. As ground cover *Geum rivale* 'Leonard'. The next morning you dash into the garden and what a pity, it was only a dream—the garden is already full! Dozens of such dreamlike combinations keep going round and round in our heads. In the riotous chapter *Wonderful* we let you share our enjoyment.

Left
From the front to the back: *Eryngium bourgatii*,
Astrantia major 'Roma' and *Allium christophii*.

Below
The border of ornamental grasses at the Oudolf
nursery. At the front, from left to right,
Eryngium giganteum, Persicaria amplexicaulis
'Firedance' and *Aster umbellatus* behind
Eupatorium maculatum 'Atropurpureum',
Foeniculum vulgare 'Giant Bronze' and
Miscanthus sinensis 'Malepartus'.

Limonium latifolium
with the inflorescences
of *Eryngium gigan-
teum* after flowering

Blazing

Here in Netherlands we live in one of those unique spots on the globe where many people would love to own an arid, dry and sunny garden. In the greatest part of the world people, in general, prefer a cooler and damper garden. One of us once experienced, in the small desert town of Marand in north-western Iran, a sudden downpour of rain in midsummer. Naturally, he dashed back into his hotel. On reaching his room, he looked out the window and, to his astonishment, saw that all the local inhabitants had run into the street . . . so, it is rather a peculiar type of person that longs for an arid, dry garden.

At the same time, people in our part of the world quickly set their hearts on a subtropical landscape. With richly flowering broom and *Cistus,* lush *Erica* and *Euphorbia,* and sweetly perfumed herbs like lavender, rosemary, and sage we conjure up a holiday landscape in the back garden. But all this is not very rational. After one cold winter your whole garden dies off and you have to start anew. For a choice of plants you can far better concentrate on places closer to home or turn your attention to eastern Europe. True, the summers there are warmer than ours, and the winters are a lot colder. But then you are assured that the plants you bring back are certainly going to survive our winters.

Closer to home, you will notice that drought-loving plants are only found in exceptional circumstances. This is logical, because our climate is neither arid nor dry. For instance, on coarse sand or gravel, both of which have no water-retentive capacities, only a few plants will grow (those that can send down their rootstock a few meters into the ground). Among these are sand sedge *(Carex arenaria),* and, occasionally, in a favorable spot, a clump of large wild thyme *(Thymus pulegioides).* Gardening becomes more enjoyable when there is a little humus in the ground: all of a sudden we see harebells *(Campanula rotundifolia),* sheep's bit *(Jasione montana),* maiden pinks *(Dianthus deltoides),* lady's bedstraw *(Galium verum),* and ling *(Calluna vulgaris).* A colorful vegetation crops up that begins to resemble what we desire in the garden—although everything still remains very small. Just a small step farther and we land in humus-rich chalky sand or sandy clay. As a rule, these are not soils with a drought-loving vegetation, except when they occur on steep southern slopes.

Now we arrive at the environment we desire in our garden. Given a blazing sun and good soil, a colorful collection of plants will thrive, for example, various *Centaurea* and *Campanula* species, meadow sage *(Salvia pratensis),* Austrian speedwell *(Veronica austriaca),* marjoram *(Origanum vulgare),* small scabious *(Scabiosa columbaria),* kidney vetch *(Anthyllis vul-*

neraria), field scabious *(Knautia arvensis),* and so forth. The result is a spectacle of color, and also insects, of which you will not quickly tire. Indeed, from the foregoing it appears that good, well-drained soil is preferable to sharp sand. In the latter case your garden will be very arid and dry but will lack the attractive planting we are discussing here that thrives best in good soil on a southern slope. Now hardly anyone has a southern slope in the garden, but a south-facing wall is no mean alternative. Apart from the grapes and kiwis that you will, undoubtedly, grow against the wall, scores of warmth-loving plants will grow at the foot of the wall. The most preferable possession in our climate is a south-facing patio or conservatory: there you can closely approach the atmosphere that is evocative of the desired southern ambience and it is not too complicated to grow tender plants.

On reading through the list of plants that follows, it strikes us just how many eastern European species appear on it: plants brought from the steppes of the Ukraine, such as *Centaurea glastifolia, Echium russicum, Limonium latifolium,* and *Phlomis tuberosa,* but also numerous plants that are found in dry and arid spots in central Germany and eastwards from there, and which are all very easy to grow in northwestern Europe. Examples are *Anemone sylvestris, Dianthus carthusianorum, Dictamnus albus, Scabiosa ochroleuca,* and *Stipa* species. (The similarity between the words *Stipa* and *steppe* can hardly be a coincidence!)

List of species

Achillea—all species
Achnatherum calamagrostis
Agastache—all species
Alcea—both species
Amsonia orientalis
Anemone sylvestris
Anthemis xhybrida 'E. C. Buxton'
Artemisia—all species except
A. lactiflora
Asphodeline lutea
Baptisia australis
Borago pygmaea
Calamintha nepeta subsp. nepeta
Centaurea benoistii
Centaurea glastifolia
Centaurea 'Pulchra Major'
Crambe maritima
Datisca cannabina
Dianthus—all species
Dictamnus albus
Echium russicum
Epilobium angustifolium
Eragrostis—all species
Eryngium—all species
Euphorbia cyparissias 'Fens Ruby'
Festuca mairei
Foeniculum vulgare
Geranium sanguineum
Glaucium corniculatum
Gypsophila altissima
Inula magnifica
Knautia macedonica
Limonium latifolium
Marrubium incanum
Origanum—all species
Panicum virgatum
Perovskia abrotanoides
Petrorhagia saxifraga
Ranunculus gramineus
Salvia argentea
Salvia officinalis
Salvia pratensis
Salvia sclarea
Scabiosa—all species

Schizachyrium scoparium
Sedum—all species
Sesleria nitida
Sporobolus heterolepis
Stipa—all species
Tanacetum corymbosum
Trifolium rubens
Verbascum lychnitis

Below
Baptisia australis

Right
Dictamnus albus
'Albiflorus'

Lush

Lush growth on fertile, moisture-retentive soil is, in reality, easier to realize in western Europe than a garden that is evocative of subtropical climes and a blazing sun. It is so easy that the majority of plants discussed in this book could be given a place in this chapter. Because of insufficient space, we shall restrict ourselves to lush vegetation in semishade and recommend, therefore, the kind of alpine plant community that the Germans so aptly call *Hochstaudenflur*. You could translate this as "a community of tall, shrublike growth" (just to let you know what we are talking about; we promise not to use such a translation again).

Above
Lunaria rediviva

Right
Podophyllum hexandrum 'Majus'

To give you an idea of what is perhaps the most beautiful collection of wild plants in Europe we shall take you to the mountains of central Europe: the Alps, Vosges, Carpathians, and the Black Forest—take your pick. The beds of the mountain valleys are filled with an extremely fertile mixture of everything that has, in the course of centuries, slid down the mountain slopes. Most of the valleys have, since time immemorial, been under cultivation, which is logical, for everything just shoots up like mad. When such valleys are mainly exploited as unfertilized hay meadows they are yellow and white with daffodils in early spring, pink with bistort *(Persicaria bistorta)* or purple with orchids in May and June. After hay-making, the scene is mainly dominated by hogweed *(Heracleum sphondylium)* and cabbage thistle *(Cirsium oleraceum)*. Only the steepest parts of such valleys have escaped deforestation. These valley beds are covered with woodlands which explode with flowering bulbs in spring.

In the fringe area between woods and natural meadows in these valleys you can come across a *Hochstaudenflur*, one of the most wonderful experiences that can happen to you during a mountain walk. Large tufts of purple monkshood *(Aconitum)* and goat's beard *(Aruncus dioicus)* thrust their way through the undergrowth that is, of course, overrun by alpine clematis *(Clematis alpina)*, hop *(Humulus lupulus)*, and fly honeysuckle *(Lonicera xylosteum)*. Here and there you will see a plume of meadow rue *(Thalictrum aquilegifolium)* interspersed with the slender inflorescence of Martagon lily *(Lilium martagon)*. Between boulders a few large clumps of blue mountain knapweed *(Centaurea montana)* or perennial cornflower, as it is sometimes called, are waiting to be admired as they grow alongside the large elliptical seeds of *Lunaria rediviva*. A few shiny, dark green leaves betray the presence of some fair maids of France *(Ranunculus aconitifolius)*, which must have colored this spot white earlier in the year. Occasionally you will see the pale green leaves of the willow gentian *(Gentiana asclepiadea)*, which only starts to flower in September. The beauty of the scene makes you want to pick up the entire plant community and move it to your own garden, but this idea is not very original, for almost all of the plants that make up the *Hochstaudenflur* are in cultivation.

The king of garden plants—which is what you could call the delphinium *(Delphinium elatum)*—is also found in the wild, be it rarely, as part of the *Hochstaudenflur*.

Obviously, this collection of plants is not limited to Europe but, in another composition, occurs in the Himalayas, central Asia, China, Japan, and North America. What is quite striking is that other parts of the world produce species that, for the most part, start to flower just when the European species have finished flowering *(Actaea, Eupatorium, Ligularia)*. By combining them, and adding the bulbous plants from the woodland valleys, a lush vegetation is created that can be in flower from February to November.

List of species

Aconitum—all species
Actaea—all species
Anemone hupehensis
Anemone xhybrida
Anemone leveillei
Anemone tomentosa
Angelica—both species
Aralia—all species
Artemisia lactiflora
Aruncus 'Horatio'
Asarum—both species
Astilbe—all species
Astilboides tabularis
Astrantia—all species
Campanula lactiflora
Cardamine waldsteinii
Carex—all species
Centaurea montana
Cephalaria gigantea
Cirsium rivulare 'Atropurpureum'
Clematis—all species
Darmera peltata
Deschampsia cespitosa

Eupatorium—all species
Euphorbia griffithii 'Dixter'
Euphorbia palustris
Filipendula—all species
Gentiana asclepiadea
Geranium 'Ann Folkard'
Geranium macrorrhizum
Geranium maculatum
Geranium Xoxonianum
Geranium palustre
Geranium phaeum
Geranium psilostemon
Geranium sylvaticum
Geum rivale
Helleborus—all species
Heuchera micrantha
Hosta—all species
Houttuynia cordata
Inula hookeri
Iris—both species
Kirengeshoma palmata
Lamium orvala
Leucanthemella serotina
Ligularia—all species
Lobelia—all species

Lunaria rediviva
Lysimachia ciliata
Lythrum—all species
Milium effusum 'Aureum'
Nepeta govaniana
Nepeta subsessilis
Persicaria—all species
Peucedanum verticillare
Podophyllum—both species
Polygonatum—all species
Pulmonaria—all species
Ranunculus aconitifolius
Rodgersia—all species
Salvia glutinosa
Sanguisorba—all species
Smyrnium perfoliatum
Stylophorum—both species
Succisa pratensis
Tanacetum macrophyllum
Thalictrum—all species
Tricyrtis—both species
Valeriana pyrenaica
Veronica longifolia
Veronicastrum virginicum

Left
Darmera peltata with
Camassia leichtlinii

Below
The shaded garden in the
Oudolf nursery with, among
others, *Smyrnium perfoliatum*
and *Lunaria rediviva*

Actaea simplex
'James Compton'

Airy

Using plants for architectural means. Perhaps you ask yourself
what is meant by this expression. For architecture and the garden . . . it is clear that the design of the garden has to do with
architecture. Paths, terraces, fences, but also shrubs and evergreens give structure to the garden in summer and winter and
can, therefore, be called architectural elements.

With perennials the structural aspects become less apparent: the plants are only around for a limited period of the year. The architectural qualities of a small number of species are obvious. Think of the large-leaved *Darmera, Hosta,* and *Rodgersia;* the sturdy, giant plants with large conspicuous inflorescences such as *Aralia and Eupatorium* species; and the number of ornamental grasses and plants with a branched candlelike growth, such as *Verbascum.* However, the architectural use of most perennial plants is not the first thing that comes to mind. But still . . . when planning a border you do generally plant the low plants at the front and the tall ones at the back. That is design. Furthermore, you take into account the shape of the plants and try to achieve the largest possible variation: spike-shaped inflorescences next to umbellifers (resembling an upturned bowl), with some rounded shapes in between. At the same time, you try to vary the kinds of foliage. The ultimate skill is to reach a certain harmony in all this variation.

We are almost inclined to exclaim: "This was lesson 1 of your gardening course," but it should be clear that the design, both for the whole as for the details, is the beginning of every successful garden. Such matters as color and atmosphere can, to a certain extent, play a role, but, generally speaking, they take second place.

A group of plants of which the architectural quality scarcely attracts attention and is, therefore, seldom or never mentioned is the group with an *airy* inflorescence. Between all the eye-catching spikes, umbels, panicles, and round-shaped plants and the "real" daisy flowers are plants with an airy inflorescence. These seem to have the modest role of being gap-fillers or, to express it more stylishly (and as such they are recognized and named), "weaving" plants. They weave the individual elements of a group of plants together, without being obvious themselves.

But just think how important they are. Tall plants with a light and airy inflorescence are not, as other tall plants, doomed to a place at the back of the border. Placed at the front of the border, strewn among shorter plants, they prevent the layout of the border from appearing stiff, and placed at the back of the border, among compact growing, tall plants, they prevent the border from appearing to close in on you. They give a natural and informal look to the border.

Borders that consist of only spikes, umbels, panicles, or round-shaped inflorescences are unthinkable, not to say ridiculous. But a border made up solely of airy plants is certainly possible in a spot where you would like to see what is actually behind the border, such as in front of a window or from the terrace.

A complete garden filled with airy plants might seem a romantic idea, but such a garden would be too unsubstantial. When there is nothing of structure between or behind the plants, the incentive to look through the plants is lacking and you are left with an indistinct haze, which rapidly becomes boring. But a garden in which there are no light and airy plants is not only lacking in romance, it is extremely uninteresting and, therefore, off-putting.

Plants with a light and airy inflorescence

Actaea simplex
Artemisia lactiflora 'Rosa Schleier'
Aruncus 'Horatio'
Cephalaria—all species
Crambe cordifolia
Foeniculum vulgare
Gypsophila altissima
Limonium latifolium
Linaria purpurea
Nepeta govaniana
Persicaria virginiana
Petrorrhagia saxifraga

Peucedanum verticillare
Pimpinella major var. rosea
Ranunculus aconitifolius
Sanguisorba officinalis
Sanguisorba 'Tanna'
Sanguisorba tenuifolia
Scabiosa ochroleuca
Silphium terebinthinaceum
Thalictrum delavayi
Thalictrum finetii
Thalictrum polygamum
Thalictrum rochebrunianum
Thalictrum 'Elin'
Verbena bonariensis

All grasses have a light and airy inflorescence; exceptionally so are the following.

Brachypodium sylvaticum
Deschampsia cespitosa
Diarrhena japonica
Eragrostis—all species
Festuca mairei
Milium effusum
Molinia caerulea var. arundinacea 'Transparent'
Panicum virgatum
Sporobolus heterolepis
Stipa gigantea

Left
Althaea 'Parkallee' and
Foeniculum vulgare 'Giant
Bronze'

Below
Sanguisorba tenuifolia
'Alba'

Filipendula rubra
'Venusta', left *Phlox*
paniculata

Tranquilllity

Tranquillity is probably that which most of us long for in these hectic times. A tranquil garden, too. We should not be shocked by what we see when we look out the window. Rather, we should feel embraced by a sense of well-being. How often does that really happen? Most gardens, as seen from the road, are unbelievably boring: a few untrimmed shrubs, a lawn the size of a handkerchief, and a large clump of *Sedum*. Let us be honest, boring is totally different from tranquil.

Sometimes our gardens are unbelievably ugly: a collection of dwarf conifers, which are neither here nor there, a blue spruce, a yellow-variegated *Chamaecyparis*, a *Forsythia* somewhere in between, and the ubiquitous clump of *Sedum*. Some gardens are gaudy, with *Alyssum, Aubrieta, Papaver, Malva,* red *Phlox,* and lots of California poppies: a kind of "hip, hip, hurray" frame of mind. We must admit that we find the latter garden sympathetic; at least something is going on and, whatever else you might think, it is certainly cheerful. But tranquil . . . we rarely see a tranquil garden that is not boring. Yet it should not be too difficult to lay out and, in our experience, many people crave such a garden.

When designing a tranquil garden the words of Goethe (*What We Bring,* 1802) are certainly applicable: "In limitations he first shows himself the master." The expression is considered by some to be a general principle when judging art. We are not of that opinion, for among the greatest works of art of all time are a number of extremely unrestrained masterpieces. But in gardening, if you wish to be surrounded by a tranquil atmosphere, it is no luxury to show some restraint.

Restraint in the design of a garden: it is obvious that a maze of paths, bits of border, lawn, or pond can hardly add up to a tranquil entity. One lawn and one border, with an unobtrusive hedge in the background, is often sufficient. A garden consisting solely of hedges and grass, without flowers, or a garden with only a pond surrounded by a hedge, are both indeed very tranquil.

Because we are writing a book on flowers we shall restrict ourselves to a garden with a border. In designing such a border you must also show restraint. Consider color. Red, orange, yellow, and white are not colors that radiate tranquilli-ty. Blue, however, is an extremely tranquil, cool color. An entire-ly blue border is so tranquil that it will lull you to sleep. Such a border has to be close to the house, otherwise you will not be able to see it. By combining blue with other, restful but warmer, colors such as lilac, purple, and pink, you will achieve a very sweet and much sought after effect. Blue, lilac, and pink, with perhaps some white or creamy yellow added, is the most popular color combination. Every owner of a garden that is open to the public will confirm that 90 percent of the visi-tors consider the blue/lilac/pink border the loveliest. So it is no wonder that clary (Salvia sclarea), which combines these three colors, is one of the most popular garden plants.

Most people long for tranquillity in their lives, in their own garden at any rate. Besides the familiar blue/lilac/pink combination, many other extremely tranquil color combinations are possibly more original. Pale yellow has a subtle and tran-quil effect and can be used with lilac or pink. Yellow with blue is a well-tried and very beautiful combination, but it does not exactly exude tranquillity.

Very attractive and perhaps not so obvious are combi-nations with green. Green with blue, for instance, is a very cool but also very charming combination. Just see how tranquil it makes you. Unusual (and tranquil) is the combination of green, pink, and widow's purple. Finally, there is the totally green gar-den, in which the nuances are sought in the shape of the foliage and in the colors. Subtle differences in inflorescence (umbelliferous, spiked, gracefully arching, or stiffly erect) play an important role in a green garden. In short, the subtle aspects are the important factors that add up to a successful, interesting green garden. The result is a super tranquil garden and, when well carried out (which is difficult), one that is defi-nitely not boring.

From the front to the back, *Stachys macran-tha* 'Robusta', *Salvia nemorosa* 'Amethyst' and *Phlomis tuberosa* 'Amazone'

Tranquil combinations

Achillea 'Hella Glashoff'
Limonium latifolium
Filipendula purpurea 'Nephele'

Gaura lindheimeri 'Whirling Butterflies'
Foeniculum vulgare 'Giant Bronze'
Perovskia abrotanoides 'Blue Spire'
Sanguisorba tenuifolia 'Alba'

Achillea 'Credo'
Nepeta govaniana
Scabiosa ochroleuca var. webbiana
Scutellaria incana
Teucrium hircanicum

Alcea rosea 'Nigra'
Monarda 'Pawnee'

Phlox paniculata
Thalictrum delavayi

Agastache rugosa
Amsonia tabernaemontana var. salicifolia
Eryngium bourgatii
Asclepias incarnata

Rudbeckia maxima

Exuberant

Not everybody is searching for tranquillity. Some like to have
a bit of spectacle in the back garden. Well, you will be thinking,
that is no problem. Bearing in mind the "hip, hip, hurray" garden mentioned in the chapter on "Tranquillity," you can advise
others to plant haphazardly in the garden, for exuberance will
almost certainly be the result. Of course, the question arises
whether this philosophy contributes towards a beautiful garden.

A list of plant names or colors does not say very much. Whether such a combination is successful or not depends on the flowering time of the various species, the height and shape of the plants, and the relationship between the individual species. In other words, which species do you put at the front, which at the back, and how many of each species do you use? And even then you are treading on thin ice when laying out an exuberant garden. There are hardly any general rules, it will always be a question of hit and miss. A combination as described above comes to you on the spur of the moment. It remains to be seen if the result is beautiful or not.

It can all be a ghastly mistake. All you can do is start over again. With a bit of luck, such a combination can be a real success. Then it is extremely satisfying to recognize that you have thought up something that you know (almost for certain) nobody has ever done before. In any case, this is what is so exciting about exuberant gardens: the big chance that it will be a flop gives you all the more satisfaction when it is a success.

This is, undoubtedly, one of the main reasons why in most of the "grand" gardens the big borders are rather exuberant. The big border is usually the showpiece of the garden, so designers are not going to just hope for the best, they will always opt for the most difficult challenge, an exuberant garden, to prove their ability. The big border in the Mien Ruys gardens in northeastern Netherlands absolutely hits you in the eye with its combination of vivid blue, orange, and yellow. Anyway, you only notice that pink, orange, white, blue, or yellow is a possibility when you actually see it accomplished. In many English gardens you will also see one exuberant border after the other. Often this is the work of the higher echelons of garden design and we understand that many will be thinking that they couldn't possible design such a border. But rest assured, these borders were not realized in one year. Moreover, we know from our own experience that, among the most sublime combinations, many have only been hit upon by mere coincidence. So do not despair, but plunge into the unknown. Try an exuberant garden. When, after many ups and downs, it is a success, you will have a very exceptional garden.

Because it is our intention to mainly talk about beautiful gardens, and we presume that an exuberant and beautiful garden can go hand in hand—otherwise this chapter would not be included in the book—it is now our task to attempt to explain how you can go about designing such a garden. Attempt, for it is not easy. For example, consider the color combination of yellowish brown, antique rose, blue, and lemon yellow. Shivers of horror will now be running down many spines. Let us elucidate: *Helenium* 'Zimbelstern', *Eupatorium cannabinum* 'Plenum', *Lobelia siphilitica,* and x*Solidaster* 'Lemore'. Many will still not be convinced that this is a beautiful combination.

Exuberant combinations

Achillea 'Walther Funcke'
Astilbe chinensis var. taquetii 'Purpurlanze'
Lobelia xgerardii 'Vedrariensis'
Monarda 'Talud'
Verbena hastata 'Rosea'

Astrantia major 'Claret'
Geranium psilostemon
Salvia nemorosa 'Tänzerin'
Delphinium elatum

Helenium autumnale 'Die Blonde'
Lobelia Xgerardii 'Vedrariensis'
Monarda 'Gardenview Scarlet'

Liatris aspera
Sedum 'Matrona'

Helenium 'Kupferzwerg'
Potentilla 'Volcan'
Salvia verticillata 'Purple Rain'
Echinacea purpurea 'Rubinglow'
Hemerocallis 'Pardon Me'

Astrantia major 'Claret'
Euphorbia griffithii 'Dixter'
Deschampsia cespitosa 'Goldtau'
Hemerocallis 'Nugget'
Monarda 'Scorpion'

Echinacea purpurea 'Rubinstern'
Digitalis ferruginea
Stachys officinalis 'Hummelo'
Sanguisorba 'Tanna'
Phlox paniculata 'Düsterlohe'

Persicaria amplexicaulis 'Firedance'
Salvia nemorosa 'Amethyst'
Achillea 'Summerwine'
Veronicastrum virginicum 'Roseum'
Panicum virgatum 'Heavy Metal'

Left
Phlox paniculata in front of *Deschampsia cespitosa* 'Goldschleier'

Below
Monarda 'Scorpion'. In the background, among others, *Deschampsia cespitosa* 'Goldschleier'.

Eryngium giganteum

Silvery

Gardening based on color is one of the most well-known and also the most obvious method. For beginners, especially, this seems to be the easiest way. Everyone can see the differences and similarities in color (unless you are color blind), and you do not seem to need a great knowledge of plants. In the previous sentences the word *seem* appears twice. *Seem* because, in practice, there are more important aspects when attempting to find a lovely combination of plants—even though you restrict yourself to one color.

Or possibly because you do want to stick to one color. For if you want to keep such a garden fascinating, then differences in structure play an important role: the shape of the flowers, the shape of the inflorescence (for example, spike, umbel, or raceme), and possibly other aspects like smell, attraction for insects, and so on.

Gardening based on color has been fully described by others, so we shall restrict ourselves to one example, a rather extreme one at that: silver. When many of us think of silver in plants, we automatically think of the color of the foliage and not the flower. (Apart from edelweiss we cannot think, off-hand, of any other silver-colored flower.) This implies that designing a garden of silvery foliage means being concerned with various flower colors. Moreover, because silver-foliaged plants do not occur frequently in the wild in our climate, a completely silver garden will soon have an unnatural effect. Finally, silver is such an extreme color that you will not want to be confronted by it in the garden year in and year out. Even indoors you only want to see it for a limited period (at Christmas).

Silver should be used to coordinate other colors. When such a color scheme is carried out well, an almost translucent atmosphere is achieved that will fascinate you for years to come. Actually, it is a widespread misunderstanding that gardening based on one color entails sticking to one color only. This would produce a dreadfully boring garden. Admittedly, in choosing silver we are stating, in perhaps an extreme fashion, that adhering to one color only is not really an option. Perhaps you are thinking that you have seen entirely white and entirely yellow gardens. Well, take another good look at the examples in the books of Elisabeth de Lestrieux. All the photographs of successful areas of gardens or arrangements based on color show that the scheme is never completely consistent. There is always a discordant note somewhere.

List of species

Achillea 'Walther Funcke'
Alchemilla conjuncta
Anemone cylindrica
Angelica sylvestris 'Vicar's Mead'
Artemisia—all species except Artemisia
  lactiflora
Asphodeline lutea
Centaurea pulchra 'Pulchra Major'
Crambe maritima
Eryngium giganteum
Eryngium yuccifolium
Geranium renardii
Glaucium corniculatum
Hosta sieboldiana 'Elegans'
Hosta xtardiana 'Blue Moon'
Hosta xtardiana 'Halcyon'

Hosta tokudama 'Hadspen Blue'
Hosta 'Blue Angel'
Hosta 'Blue Impression'
Hosta 'Krossa Regal'
Lamium maculatum 'White Nancy'
Linaria purpurea
Lysimachia ephemerum
Marrubium incanum
Panicum virgatum 'Cloud Nine'
Panicum virgatum 'Dallas Blues'
Panicum virgatum 'Heavy Metal'
Perovskia abrotanoides 'Little Spire'
Phlomis russeliana
Pulmonaria 'Majeste'
Ranunculus gramineus
Rudbeckia maxima

Salvia argentea
Salvia officinalis 'Berggarten'
Sanguisorba armena
Sanguisorba 'Tanna'
Schizachyrium scoparium
Scutellaria incana
Sedum telephium subsp. ruprechtii
Sesleria nitida
Sorghastrum nutans 'Sioux Blue'
Stipa pulcherrima
Thalictrum flavum subsp. glaucum
Thalictrum rochebruneanum
Thalictrum 'Elin'
Verbascum lychnitis
Veronica spicata 'Spitzentraum'

Left
Sorghastrum nutans 'Sioux
Blue' (right) and *Atriplex
hortensis* var. *rubra*

Below
The ribbed foliage of *Crambe
maritima*; right a *Phlox* hybrid

Grassy

Grassy meadows, ungrassy gardens. Apart from lawns, grasses still do not play an important role in most gardens. Why? Probably because 90 percent of all that grows and flowers around us is grass and is, therefore, not exciting enough for us to want to have it in the garden as well. Or, is it that we are not used to the idea of planting grass in the garden because it is attractive and because we do not know how to go about it? Probably the latter is the case.

Stipa turkestanica with, among others, *Foeniculum vulgare* 'Giant Bronze'

In the introduction to this book we mentioned the tendency towards more natural gardening. This tendency leads us to expect that more people are using ornamental grasses in their gardens. We are seeing it happen. Interest in ornamental grasses has increased, but, apart from a clump of grass here and there, you cannot state that the use of ornamental grasses has now become general practice. The tradition that a garden should, in the first place, consist of flowers is sometimes more tenacious than we care for. Flowers can only play a principal part in the garden for a few months. During the rest of the year, shape and structure are important, the structure of inanimate elements like fences and paths and the shape of animate shrubs and hedges. But what about the large spaces between them?

To keep the garden space designated for flowers exciting throughout the year, grasses are often indispensable. At all levels—ornamental grasses can vary in height from 10 cm to 2 1/2 m—grasses can be used as elements of design or coordination. Two aspects of grasses are important here. First, the large round clumps are especially wonderful architectural elements in an autumn and winter garden. Second, the inflorescences in spring and summer are almost always light and airy and, therefore, play an important role in opening up rather solid masses of color among the flowering plants.

The ornamental grass garden

Whoever ventures a step further will arrive at a garden that is made up mainly or exclusively of grasses. This kind of garden is possible because there is enough variety among the different species. But how do you go about achieving such a garden? Both of us have been fascinated by the idea for years. While considering the possibility, you may quickly hit upon the idea of taking a look at how nature copes in situations where grasses have the upper hand. Not the meadows under cultivation, as we know them here—they are not wild but the product of human intervention—but the purely natural grasslands of the North American prairie, the Argentinian pampas, the South African veldt, and the steppes of Europe and Asia.

Is it feasible to capture something of the atmosphere of these wide open spaces, which stretch from horizon to horizon, in the restricted area of a garden? Well no, and yet again, yes. No, because you cannot restrict infinite space and you would not want the monotony of that landscape in your garden, anyway. Give it a try and you will end up making the same mistakes the originators of the heather garden made. Yes, because when you look at the details you can learn something from the structural composition of such grasslands. Within the predominant framework of the various species of grasses you will notice that numerous flowering plants appear. In early spring all varieties of violets and bulbous plants are in flower among the half-decayed debris of the previous year. In summer, tall-growing plants, such as *Lupinus, Amsonia, Phlomis, Limonium, Papaver,* and *Echinacea,* which have been able to keep pace with the growing grass, just manage to catch sufficient sunlight to bring forth flowers—often in very eye-catching colors. In late summer and autumn, the very tall species of *Aster, Vernonia, Helianthus,* and *Silphium* add color to the flaming autumn shades of the many grasses that are then at their zenith. This is how a border of grasses is built up.

We will show you an example. When designing a border of grasses, it is not necessary to use only those flowering plants that appear in the grasslands of the world. As we mentioned earlier, there is no point in copying these grasslands because you cannot capture the atmosphere of such a landscape. Delphiniums, which never occupy a place in wild grasslands, fit in sublimely with grasses: the heavy flowering racemes combine perfectly with the lax plumes of the grasses.

A garden planted exclusively with grasses is a completely different option. Grasses have such a strong architectural effect that you must try to avoid the garden becoming rigid and artificial. This is not a problem when designing a garden for an office building, because such a garden is, in the first place, something to gaze upon; it is not a garden to be lived in. We would tackle a private garden in a totally different manner. For instance, by restricting ourselves to a small number of species, and putting the available space to logical use, we can create a peaceful garden that evokes a sense of well-being.

It can also be fascinating to reserve the garden or part of the garden for man-sized grasses and various species of bamboo. Such a garden gives you the impression of being in a mountain forest in southern China (where you could come face to face with a giant panda at any moment) and this could have a tranquilizing and, at the same time, oppressive effect. A garden of tall grasses and bamboos is at its best when, after a good downpour, all the plants are dripping wet. So you see, such a garden would fit perfectly well into our climate.

Summing up, grasses can be put to many uses other than for lawns, many more than we can discuss in this chapter. Should you have become more enthusiastic for grasses, then we are immensely satisfied.

Left
Calamagrostis brachytricha in front of *Perovskia abrotanoides* 'Little Spire' and *Veronicastrum* 'Temptation' in the RHS gardens at Wisley

Below
Achnatherum calamagrostis and *Aconitum lamarckii*

Gloomy?

When the last flowers disappear from the garden at the end of autumn a gloomy period sets in for many people. The dying plants are cut down and all the debris is raked up and disposed of. The result is a horrendous landscape that faces a long, deadly winter in which rain, wind, and frost can play havoc mercilessly. Indeed, very gloomy! Gloomy for all the birds that are still around in winter; they will avoid such a garden because it has nothing edible in it. And gloomy for the owner, who is obliged to sit with his or her back to the window for the next few months because there is no garden to look at.

Above
Euphorbia palustris in autumn

Right
Darmera peltata in autumn glory

Happily, more and more gardeners are becoming convinced that their gardens should not be tidied-up for the winter, that they would rather enjoy watching the birds rummage around the garden for seeds or insects that have sought refuge in dead stalks or under the fallen leaves, and that they would also rather enjoy the garden when it is transformed into a winter fairyland by frost and snow.

Not all perennial plants remain equally attractive in winter. Some soon disintegrate and others change into a pile of pulp after the first night frost, but enough proudly remain erect throughout winter, or for the greater part of it, and retain their interesting shape with or without frost or snow. These include not only the plants that flower in late summer or autumn, but also a surprising number of plants that flower in early summer. Moreover, many perennials have foliage that turns a flaming autumn color before it falls to the ground. Who said something about gloomy?

Plants with beautiful autumn colors

Amsonia hubrichtii
Amsonia tabernaemontana var. *salicifolia*
Aruncus 'Horatio'
Baptisia australis
Calamagrostis brachytricha
Ceratostigma plumbaginoides
Darmera peltata
Epilobium angustifolium
Eupatorium maculatum

Euphorbia cyparissias
Euphorbia palustris
Euphorbia schillingii
Gaura lindheimeri
Geranium soboliferum
Geranium wlassovianum
Gillenia trifoliata
Hakonechloa macra
Hemerocallis—all species
Hosta—all species
Limonium latifolium
Miscanthus—all species

Molinia—all species
Panicum virgatum
Polygonatum—all species
Sanguisorba canadensis
Sanguisorba 'Tanna'
Schizachyrium scoparium
Silphium terebinthinaceum
Sporobolus heterolepis
Thalictrum aquilegifolium
Thalictrum delavayi
Thalictrum polygamum
Verbena hastata

Below
The seeds of *Asclepias incarnata*

Right
Eupatorium maculatum 'Atropurpureum' and *Molinia caerulea* var. *arundinacea* 'Transparent' in winter.

Plants with beautiful winter silhouettes

Agastache—all species
Aruncus 'Horatio'
Aster lateriflorus 'Horizontalis'
Aster umbellatus
Astilbe—all species
Calamagrostis xacutiflora 'Karl Foerster'
Deschampsia cespitosa
Digitalis ferruginea
Digitalis parviflora
Echinacea purpurea
Eryngium—all species
Eupatorium—all species
Filipendula—all species
Foeniculum vulgare

Glycyrrhiza yunnanensis
Hosta—all species
Kirengeshoma palmata
Liatris—all species
Ligularia—all species
Limonium latifolium
Lunaria rediviva
Lythrum virgatum
Marrubium incanum
Miscanthus—all species
Molinia caerulea
Monarda—all species
Origanum—all species
Panicum virgatum 'Dallas Blues'
Panicum virgatum 'Cloud Nine'
Pennisetum—all species
Perovskia abrotanoides

Peucedanum verticillare
Phlomis—all species
Rodgersia—all species
Rudbeckia—both species
Scutellaria incana
Sedum—all species
Serratula seoanei
Stachys officinalis
Stipa—all species
Teucrium hircanicum
Thalictrum polygamum
Veratrum californicum
Verbascum lychnitis
Verbena hastata
Vernonia crinita
Veronica longifolia
Veronicastrum virginicum

Autumn

When you look through the long list of autumn-flowering plants you will wonder why most gardens are so utterly boring in autumn, and perhaps why your garden is so boring in autumn, too. In the introductory chapters on plant uses we explained why this is: in spring, you overenthusiastically run outside and fill up all the space with spring-flowering plants, so that there is no space left for the autumn flowers. "Big mistake!" we added, most sternly.

Above
The transience of life shown at its best in the Priona gardens: the "borrowed" landscape in the background is no more. It has been dismantled by the neighbors and replaced by a conifer hedge.

Right
Sanguisorba officinalis 'Red Thunder' and *Molinia caerulea* var. *arundinacea* 'Transparent'

To show that we are not only strict but also honest, we share the following anecdote. When we initially wrote this section at the end of January 1990, we were experiencing the umpteenth mild winter. Outside, the witch hazels, snowdrops, *Crocus sieberi* and *C. chrysanthus*, *Viburnum* X*bodnantense* 'Dawn', *Sarcococca humilis,* and *Helleborus foetidus* were in flower, while other *Helleborus* species were about to burst into flower. It was only with the utmost self-control that we forced ourselves to stay indoors—otherwise we might never have finished this book! We would have much rather dashed outside and started on the big spring clean-up in the garden to get a better view of the flowering bulbs. That would have been a big mistake, for it can be awfully cold in February. So you see, we too lack patience as do all other garden lovers, and we can sympathize. (Note: As we are putting the finishing touches to the revised edition of this book, mid-February 2003, we are experiencing a very sharp frost and outside nothing at all is in flower. Yet, we are still enjoying to the full the winter silhouettes in the garden. All the more reason for us to add a section to this book titled "Gloomy?")

The strong desire for flowers that besets us in spring can, for the most part, be satisfied with bulbs and shrubs that flower in spring. If we agree to plant late summer-flowering and autumn-flowering plants in most of the spots that were designated for spring-flowering plants, then we shall be on the right road to success. We are presuming that the summer flower situation is OK and that an occasional tuft of lungwort or *Primula* cannot do much harm.

Back to autumn: this is when nature comes to full maturity. The last perennials reach their full height, berries and seeds are ripening on others. While the foliage colors deepen to flaming orange, yellow, and red, the colors of the (many, see list) autumn flowers become softer. The season of mist and autumn adds that little extra to the scene. At the same time, amid this surplus of good feeling, *la grande bouffe* is getting under way as hordes of insects enjoy a first-rate meal, lapping up the last of the nectar and gobbling their way through the dying stalks and leaves. The biggest gluttons, the butterflies, reach their peak in August and stay around until November. And legions of garden spiders, in their turn, decimate the hordes of hovering insects. In the meantime, the tits, greenfinches, chaffinches, twites, and goldfinches gather around to partake of the banquet. And in your garden would you have none of this because you had partaken of too much in spring? Come on now!

Autumn-flowering plants

Aconitum carmichaelii var. wilsonii
Aconitum episcopale
Actaea cordifolia
Actaea japonica
Actaea mairei
Actaea simplex
Anemone hupehensis
Anemone tomentosa
Anemone xhybrida
Artemisia lactiflora
Aster cordifolius
Aster ericoides
Aster laevis
Aster lateriflorus
Aster novae-angliae
Aster umbellatus
Aster hybrids
Calamagrostis brachytricha
Calamintha nepeta subsp. nepeta
Ceratostigma plumbaginoides

Chasmantium latifolium
Clematis heracleifolia 'China Purple'
Clematis jouiniana
Coreopsis tripteris
Dendranthema—all species
Eragrostis spectabilis
Eragrostis trichodes
Eupatorium—all species
Gentiana asclepiadea
Glycyrrhiza yunnanensis
Helenium—all species
Helianthus—all species
Hosta plantaginea 'Grandiflora'
Kalimeris pinnatifida 'Hortensis'
Kirengeshoma palmata
Leucanthemella serotina
Miscanthus—all species
Molinia—all species
Origanum laevigatum
Panicum—all species
Pennisetum—all species

Perovskia abrotanoides 'Blue Spire'
Persicaria campanulata
Rudbeckia maxima
Salvia azurea
Salvia glutinosa
Sanguisorba canadensis
Sanguisorba officinalis 'Red Thunder'
Saxifraga cortusifolia
Scutellaria incana
Sedum—all species
Serratula seoanei
Silphium—all species
Solidago—all species
xSolidaster luteus
Sorghastrum nutans
Strobilanthes atropurpureus
Succisella inflexa
Tricyrtis—all species
Verbesina alternifolia
Vernonia crinita

Summer-flowering plants that continue to flower into autumn

Achillea 'Summerwine'
Agastache—both species
Alcea—all species
Anthemis 'E. C. Buxton'
Aster amellus
Aster divaricatus
Aster xfrikartii 'Mönch'
Aster macrophyllus 'Twilight'
Borago pygmaea
Cirsium rivulare 'Atropurpureum'
Delphinium all remontant species
Dianthus amurensis
Echinacea—all species
Euphorbia schillingii

Foeniculum vulgare
Gaura lindheimeri
Geranium nodosum
Geranium xoxonianum
Geranium soboliferum
Geranium wallichianum 'Buxton's Variety'
Geranium 'Dilys'
Geranium wlassovianum
Glaucium corniculatum
Kalimeris incisa
Lamium maculatum
Lavatera—all species
Ligularia veitchiana
Linaria purpurea
Lysimachia ephemerum

Nepeta govaniana
Origanum vulgare
Penstemon barbatus 'Praecox Nanus'
Persicaria amplexicaulis
Persicaria virginiana
Petrorhagia saxifraga
Phlox paniculata 'Lichtspel'
Salvia verticillata
Scabiosa ochroleuca
Selinum wallichianum
Sidalcea—all species
Sporobolus heterolepis
Teucrium hircanicum
Verbena bonariensis
Viola cornuta

Left
Verbesina alternifolia

Below
In the foreground Persicaria amplexicaulis 'Rosea', behind, among others, Vernonia crinita 'Mammuth' and Viburnum nudum (left).

Wonderful

Almost everyone knows the feeling the first time you see the Alps or the Rocky Mountains: ooh, my goodness, aren't they high? And how impressive! Later in life, in even more blessed spots like eastern Turkey, the Andes, or the Himalayas, you recapture that feeling, but twice as intensely. The first time you visit one of the famous gardens, such as Sissinghurst or Hadspen House, you experience the same: oooh, unbelievable!

Behind a group of *Monarda* hybrids is pale yellow *Thalictrum lucidum*

And, at the risk of appearing immodest, you may have a similar experience when visiting the garden of Piet and Anja Oudolf and my own plantings at the Priona gardens, for we are still busy thinking up and planting "wonderful" combinations that give you the same "oooh!" feeling. Many of the breathtaking combinations that you can see in our gardens, or in others, are not necessarily based on the principles set out in the previous chapters. Ecology, architecture, atmosphere, color, and shape all play a role, but no one factor is all-important.

In the combination of *Carex pendula, Persicaria amplexicaulis* 'Firedance', *Filipendula rubra* 'Venusta', and *Geum rivale* 'Leonard', ecology plays a part in that all these plants enjoy good, water-retentive soil. But, *Persicaria amplexicaulis,* which hails from the Himalayas, prefers a dry climate in winter. The result is that the combination is only possible if the soil is water-retentive and well-drained, because *Persicaria* will rot if her roots are in stagnant ground water during the winter. The other three species often have their feet in water during the winter, but from our (garden) experience it appears that this is not an absolute necessity: they also thrive in well-drained soil. Ecologically, then, this combination is not 100 percent sound, but in practice it appears to perform well on ordinary, humus-rich garden soil. And that is, of course, the main thing.

Color is another important principle here. The flowers of three of the plants are pink/red and the fourth is a shade of brown. Thus, they are a good match. How architecture and design have been dealt with in this combination can best be illustrated by picturing in your mind what a sketch of the planting might look like. Rough as it is, the sketch makes it clear how the various species compare in shape and where each of them has to be planted. Picture three large mopheads of *Carex pendula* and a big patch of the narrow, spike-shaped *Persicaria.* Behind are the tall, fluffy plumes of *Filipendula* and, in between, the attractive foliage of *Geum rivale,* which finishes flowering in the summer. To determine how many plants of each species are needed, simply transfer the sketch to a blueprint.

Now that you know the tricks of the trade it only remains for us to present you with a number of wonderful, mouth-watering combinations. We would like to explain how they came about. An unsuspecting passer-by would probably have declared us to be crazy. Imagine two men holding a conversation in Latin. The first one says, "*Helenium* 'Rubinkuppel' with *Echinacea* 'White Lustre'" and the other agrees, "Yes, that orange center together with the brownish-red flowers, magnificent! And then some purple-blue dotted in between . . . *Salvia* perhaps?"

"Well, that's not really very out-of-the-ordinary . . . let me think . . . what about *Perovskia?*"

"Wow, that's fantastic" is the answer (we are both in our fifties, our excuse for using the hopelessly old-fashioned sixties' jargon). "And then if we have a mass of *Nepeta govaniana* hanging in between?"

"Yes!" (Imagine the left-hand wildly waving back and forth.) "Yes, that's it. Really lovely. Wonderful! We'll stick to this."

This comedy act for two gentlemen continued throughout the day and produced, besides many oooooh's and aaaaah's, the following "wonderful" combinations:

"Wonderful" combinations

Astrantia major 'Claret'
Geranium xoxonianum 'Rose Clair'
Hosta 'Blue Impression'
Molopospermum peloponnesiacum
Digitalis parviflora

Deschampsia cespitosa 'Goldtau'
Astilbe chinensis var. taquetii
 'Purpurlanze'
Astrantia major 'Roma'
Gillenia trifoliata
Molinia caerulea var. arundinacea
 'Transparent'

Achillea 'Hella Glashoff'
Digitalis ferruginea
Eryngium giganteum
Origanum vulgare 'Rosenkuppel'
Sesleria nitida

Achillea 'Walther Funcke'
Hemerocallis 'Green Flutter'
Selinum wallichianum
Echinacea pallida

Monarda 'Talud'
Verbena hastata
Aster macrophyllus 'Twilight'
Sporobolus heterolepis
Salvia verticillata 'Purple Rain'

Calamagrostis xacutiflora 'Karl Foerster'
Nepeta subsessilis
Filipendula rubra 'Venusta'
Sanguisorba officinalis 'Arnhem'
Delphinium elatum

Foeniculum vulgare 'Giant Bronze'
Persicaria amplexicaulis 'Firedance'
Sanguisorba tenuifolia 'Alba'
Miscanthus 'Zwergelefant'
Thalictrum lucidum

Sporobolus heterolepis
Origanum vulgare 'Rosenkuppel'
Limonium latifolium
Trifolium rubens

Briza media 'Limouzi'
Geranium psilostemon
Hosta 'Halcyon'
Salvia nemorosa 'Blauhügel'
Geum rivale 'Leonard'

Amsonia tabernaemontana var. salicifolia
Agastache rugosa 'Blue Fortune'
Stachys officinalis 'Rosea'
Salvia verticillata 'Purple Rain'
Knautia dipsacifolia

Below
Angelica gigas (left),
Datisca cannabina
(right)

Right
From left to right a
pink *Lobelia* hybrid,
Echinacea purpurea
'Rubinglow' and
Helenium
'Kupferzwerg';
behind *Sanguisorba
officinalis* 'Red
Thunder' and *Molinia
caerulea* var. *arundi-
nacea* 'Transparent'

Sesleria nitida
Salvia nemorosa 'Mainacht'
Stachys officinalis 'Hummelo'
Pimpinella major var. *rosea'*
Potentilla xhopwoodiana

Lavatera cachemiriana 'White Angel'
Monarda 'Fishes'
Phlox paniculata 'Rosa Pastell'
Potentilla thurberi

Achillea 'Summerwine'
Dianthus carthusianorum
Linaria purpurea
Pennisetum viridescens
Sidalcea oregana 'My Love'

Anemone tomentosa 'Robustissima'
Actaea simplex 'James Compton'
Eupatorium maculatum 'Atropurpureum'

Molinia caerulea var. *arundinacea*
 'Transparent'
Aster novae-angliae 'Violetta'

Leucanthemella serotina
Eupatorium maculatum 'Atropurpureum'
Molinia caerulea var. *arundinacea*
 'Karl Foerster'
Salvia azurea
Sporobolus heterolepis

Trifolium rubens 'Peach Pink'
Perovskia abrotanoides 'Little Spire'
Sedum telephium subsp. *maximum*
 'Purple Emperor'
Limonium latifolium

Echinacea purpurea 'Rubinglow'
Agastache rugosa
Liatris ligulistylis
Helenium 'Rubinzwerg'
Amsonia hubrichtii

Stachys officinalis 'Hummelo'
Molinia caerulea 'Poul Peterson'
Sanguisorba menziesii
Astrantia major 'Roma'
Geranium soboliferum

Salvia nemorosa 'Evelyn'
Eragrostis curvula
Hemerocallis 'Joan Senior'
Eryngium yuccifolium

Anemone xhybrida 'Honorine Jobert'
Eupatorium maculatum 'Purple Bush'
Panicum virgatum 'Dallas Blues'
Aster amellus 'Sonora'
Phlomis tuberosa 'Amazone'

Deschampsia cespitosa 'Goldschleier'
Euphorbia griffithii 'Dixter'
Hemerocallis 'Green Flutter'
Stachys officinalis 'Rosea'
Asclepias incarnata

Good Neighbors

This book mentions many unfamiliar plants that are, therefore, only to be seen in a few gardens. So, in actual practice, it is difficult to pick up ideas for combinations. That is why we have given a comprehensive description of the various uses. In spite of this we can imagine that you still do not know what you can do with the different species. This particularly applies to some species that do not immediately catch the eye. Yet these are the species that are often indispensable when creating beautiful combinations. We have, therefore, included those species and most grasses in the list of ideas for combinations. When putting these combinations together we have considered that they flower at the same time and have the same ecological requirements. The species also match as far as shape and color are concerned. They are not ideas for complete borders but first small steps towards what could become a wonderful border.

Actaea pachypoda
Carex grayi
Euphorbia griffithii 'Dixter'
Heuchera micrantha
Hosta sieboldiana 'Elegans'

Alchemilla erythropoda
Geranium xoxonianum
Hosta tokudama 'Hadspen Blue'
Geum rivale 'Leonard'
Gillenia trifoliata

Amsonia orientalis
Centaurea glastifolia
Tanacetum corymbosum
Salvia hians

Amsonia tabernaemontana var. *salicifolia*
Aconitum lamarckii
Anemone levellei
Deschampsia cespitosa

Anemone sylvestris
Dianthus carthusianorum
Limonium latifolium
Scabiosa lucida
Stipa turkestanica

Anemone cylindrica
Achillea 'Hella Glashoff'
Platycodon grandiflorus 'Perlmutterschale'
Spodiopogon sibiricus
Sanguisorba 'Tanna'

Asphodeline lutea
Amsonia orientalis
Baptisia australis
Sesleria nitida
Thalictrum flavum subsp. *glaucum*

Aster macrophyllus 'Twilight'
Geranium nodosum
Gillenia trifoliata
Scutellaria incana
Thalictrum delavayi

Aster umbellatus
Eupatorium maculatum 'Atropurpureum'
Miscanthus sinensis 'Malepartus'
Persicaria amplexicaulis
Verbesina alternifolia

Baptisia australis
Achillea 'Hella Glashoff'

Amsonia orientalis
Eryngium giganteum
Salvia nemorosa 'Tänzerin'

Calamintha nepeta subsp. *nepeta*
Gaura lindheimeri 'Whirling Butterflies'
Liatris spicata 'Alba'
Perovskia abrotanoides 'Blue Spire'
Sedum telephium subsp. *maximum* 'Atropurpureum'

Cirsium rivulare 'Atropurpureum'
Centaurea montana 'Carnea'
Deschampsia cespitosa 'Goldschleier'
Filipendula purpurea
Geranium sylvaticum 'Amy Doncaster'

Galega orientalis
Astilbe chinensis var. *taquetii* 'Purpurlanze'
Delphinium elatum
Lychnis chalcedonica 'Carnea'

Gillenia trifoliata
Astrantia major 'Roma'
Geranium phaeum 'Springtime'
Thalictrum delavayi 'Album'

Kalimeris incisa
Cirsium rivulare 'Atropurpureum'
Digitalis ferruginea
Salvia nemorosa 'Tänzerin'
Sanguisorba menziesii

Kirengeshoma palmata
Actaea simplex 'James Compton'
Anemone tomentosa 'Albadura'
Thalictrum finetii

Lamium orvala
Carex muskingumensis
Heuchera micrantha 'Palace Purple'
Mertensia sibirica

Lindelofia anchusoides
Astrantia major
Digitalis grandiflora
Geranium psilostemon
Thalictrum aquilegifolium

Lunaria rediviva
Aquilegia flabellata
Geranium maculatum
Persicaria bistorta subsp. *carnea*
Viola elatior

Nepeta govaniana
Achillea 'Summerwine'
Lysimachia ephemerum
Monarda 'Oudolf's Charm'
Perovskia abrotanoides 'Blue Spire'

Phlomis tuberosa 'Amazone'
Crambe cordifolia
Geranium psilostemon
Lychnis chalcedonica 'Carnea'

Rudbeckia maxima
Agastache rugosa
Asclepias incarnata
Sedum telephium 'Matrona'

Sanguisorba tenuifolia 'Alba'
Filipendula rubra 'Venusta Magnifica'
Monarda 'Pawnee'
Phlox paniculata 'Lichtspel'

Scabiosa ochroleuca
Monarda 'Scorpion'
Scutellaria incana
Sedum telephium subsp. maximum
  'Atropurpureum'

Selinum wallichianum
Eupatorium maculatum 'Atropurpureum'
Sanguisorba officinalis 'Red Thunder'
Veronicastrum virginicum 'Roseum'

Smyrnium perfoliatum
Lamium orvala
Lunaria rediviva
Ranunculus aconitifolius
Polygonatum xhybridum
  'Weihenstephan'

Solidago caesia
Aster xfrikartii 'Mönch'
Succisella inflexa
Trycyrtis formosana

Stachys officinalis 'Rosea'
Achillea 'Lilac Beauty'
Geranium wlassovianum
Salvia nemorosa 'Dear Anja'

Tanacetum macrophyllum
Aconitum napellus
Campanula lactiflora
Geranium phaeum 'Lily Lovell'
Thalictrum aquilegifolium

Trachystemon orientalis
Geranium macrorrhizum 'Album'
Pulmonaria longifolia
Tiarella wherryi

Vernonia crinita
Aster novae-angliae 'Violetta'
Leucanthemella serotina
Molinia caerulea var. arundinacea
  'Karl Foerster'
Polygonum amplexicaule 'Firetail'
Salvia azurea

Ornamental Grasses

Brachypodium sylvaticum
Euphorbia coralloides
Hosta 'Blue Angel'
Thalictrum delavayi

Briza media 'Limouzi'
Alchemilla conjuncta
Eryngium bourgatii
Stachys officinalis
Viola cornuta

Calamagrostis xacutiflora 'Karl Foerster'
Echinacea purpurea
Eupatorium maculatum 'Atropurpureum'
Phlox paniculata 'Lavendelwolke'

Calamagrostis brachytricha
Echinacea purpurea
Kalimeris incisa
Lavatera cachemiriana
Origanum vulgare 'Rosenkuppel'

Carex muskingumensis
Astilbe chinensis var. taquetii
  'Purpurlanze'
Aster xfrikartii 'Mönch'
Persicaria amplexicaulis 'Rosea'

Sanguisorba 'Tanna'
Chasmantium latifolium
Aster lateriflorus 'Horizontalis'
Lysimachia ephemerum
Panicum virgatum 'Rehbraun'
Sanguisorba canadensis

Deschampsia cespitosa 'Goldschleier'
Astrantia major 'Claret'
Campanula 'Burghaltii'
Digitalis parviflora
Lobelia siphilitica

Hakonechloa macra 'Aureola'
Dictamnus albus
Scutellaria incana
Tricyrtis formosana

Milium effusum 'Aureum'
Epimedium xversicolor 'Sulphureum'
Helleborus odorus
Hosta sieboldiana 'Frances Williams'
Viola labradorica

Miscanthus sinensis 'Kleine Silberspinne'
Datisca cannabina
Helenium 'Rubinkuppel'
Lobelia xgerardii 'Vedrariensis'
Perovskia abrotanoides 'Blue Spire'

Miscanthus sinensis 'Malepartus'
Aster cordifolius 'Little Carlow'
Coreopsis tripteris
Eupatorium purpureum ' Album'
Vernonia crinita

Molinia caerulea 'Moorhexe'
Asclepias incarnata
Knautia dipsacifolia
Salvia nemorosa
Sanguisorba menziesii

Molinia caerulea var. arundinacea
  'Transparent'
Eupatorium maculatum 'Atropurpureum'
Monarda 'Cherokee'
Salvia sclarea
Veronicastrum virginicum 'Fascination'

Panicum virgatum 'Cloud Nine'
Agastache rugosa
Amsonia hubrichtii
Echinacea pallida
Rudbeckia occidentalis

Panicum virgatum 'Rehbraun'
Aster cordifolius 'Little Carlow'
Selinum wallichianum
xSolidaster luteus 'Lemore'
Sorghastrum nutans 'Sioux Blue'

Sesleria nitida
Achillea 'Walther Funcke'
Geranium xoxonianum
Polemonium 'Lambrook Manor'
Salvia nemorosa 'Blauhügel'

Sorghastrum nutans
Actaea simplex 'Scimitar'
Anemone xhybrida 'Honorine Jobert'
Eupatorium rugosum
Persicaria campanulata

Spodiopogon sibiricus
Aconitum carmichaelii var. wilsonii
Persicaria virginiana
Salvia glutinosa

Sporobolus heterolepis
Agastache rugosa
Amsonia hubrichtii
Eryngium yuccifolium
Geranium soboliferum
Trifolium rubens

Stipa gigantea
Baptisia australis
Tanacetum corymbosum
Salvia nemorosa 'Dear Anja'
Veronicastrum 'Temptation'

Stipa pulcherrima
Achillea 'Summerwine'
Anthemis xhybrida 'E. C. Buxton'
Agastache rugosa 'Blue Fortune'

A "Blazing" border

Design: Henk Gerritsen

1M.   2M.   3M.

A "Lush" border

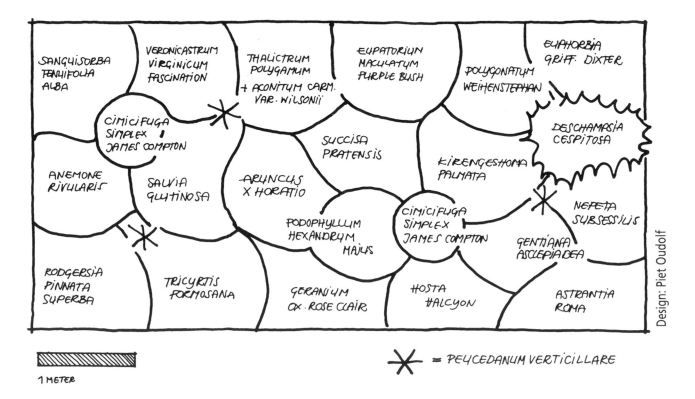

Design: Piet Oudolf

1 METER

✳ = PEUCEDANUM VERTICILLARE

An autumn border

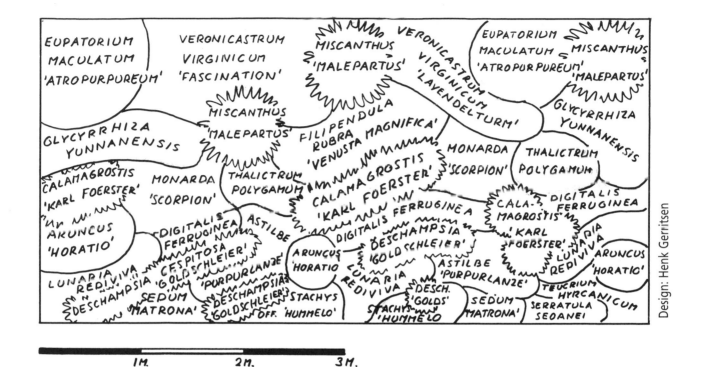

Design: Henk Gerritsen

An ornamental grasses border

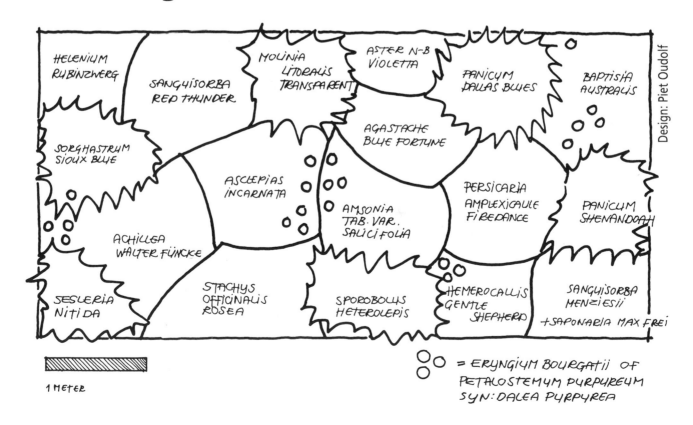

Design: Piet Oudolf

Aconitum napellus 'Stainless Steel'

Exceptional Properties of Plants

In gardening you can come across far more possibilities and/or problems than we have been able to deal with in the preceding chapters on uses. Perhaps you live at the coast or your garden is overrun by rabbits. Perhaps you want a lovely garden but cannot stand gardening. Or would you like a garden especially for butterflies? Here follow a few lists of plants that fit in with such specific wishes or problems. Only plants that appear in the plant descriptions of this book are mentioned.

Short-lived plants

Biennials or short-lived perennials can present an insurmountable problem for some people because everything that dies off and disappears involves extra work in the garden. Such plants are attractive to the gardener, however, because they (usually) self-seed profusely and keep reappearing in other spots in the garden. As a result, the garden looks different each year.

Achillea—all species
Agastache—all species
Alcea—all species
Angelica—all species
Anthemis 'E. C. Buxton'
Aquilegia—all species
Borago pygmaea
Brachypodium sylvaticum
Digitalis—all species
Echium russicum
Eryngium giganteum
Euphorbia coralloides
Foeniculum vulgare
Gaura lindheimeri
Glaucium corniculatum
Helleborus foetidus
Linaria purpurea
Lobelia—all species

Achillea 'Hella Glashoff'

Hemerocallis—all species
Hosta—all species
Inula magnifica
Lamium orvala
Lunaria rediviva
Miscanthus—all species
Molinia—all species
Persicaria amplexicaulis
Persicaria polymorpha
Polygonatum—all species
Sesleria nitida
Silphium—all species
Solidago rugosa

Phlox paniculata 'Lichtspel'

Nepeta clarkei
Peucedanum verticillare
Salvia argentea
Salvia sclarea
Scabiosa ochroleuca
Smyrnium perfoliatum
Teucrium hircanicum
Verbascum lychnitis
Verbena–all species

Plants for lazy gardeners

People who would like a beautiful garden but are not prepared to work in it had better pave it. There is hope on the horizon for those who are prepared to do a tiny bit of work: the following plants are strong enough to keep alive without too much upkeep. This does not imply that you can just plunk them between the stinging nettles. That is asking too much. However, once the plants are established and have reached maturity, they can survive and almost go it alone.

Amsonia tabernaemontana var. *salicifolia*
Aralia californica
Aster divaricatus
Aster macrophyllus 'Twilight'
Aster umbellatus
Calamagrostis xacutiflora 'Karl Foerster'
Carex pendula
Cephalaria gigantea
Darmera peltata
Deschampsia cespitosa
Echinops sphaerocephalus
Eupatorium—all species
Euphorbia griffithii 'Dixter'
Euphorbia palustris
Filipendula kamtschatica
Filipendula rubra 'Venusta'
Geranium macrorrhizum
Geranium nodosum
Geranium phaeum
Geranium pratense
Helianthus—all species

Geranium sylvaticum 'Amy Doncaster'

Spodiopogon sibiricus
Thalictrum polygamum
Verbesina alternifolia
Veronicastrum virginicum

The saggers and the stakers

Of course, there are gardeners who cannot get enough of it. Such people naturally choose lots of delphiniums because that gives them something to do. There are many more such plants that sag and need to be staked, supported by brushwood, or cut back before the longest day.

Aconitum lamarckii
Artemisia ludoviciana var. *latiloba*
Aster xfrikartii 'Mönch'
Campanula 'Burghaltii'
Campanula 'Kent Belle'
Clematis integrifolia
Clematis xjouiniana
Clematis recta
Delphinium—all species
Geranium pratense
Gypsophila altissima
Knautia dipsacifolia
Knautia macedonica
Nepeta sibirica
Phlox paniculata
Rudbeckia maxima
Salvia azurea

Sanguisorba officinalis 'Red Thunder'
Sanguisorba tenuifolia
Thalictrum aquilegifolium
Thalictrum delavayi
Thalictrum flavum subsp. *glaucum*
Trifolium rubens
Veronicastrum virginicum

Plants in need of support

There is a solution for those people who are not inclined to do much in the garden but who are, at the same time, mad about plants that sag and need staking: plant them between sturdy, bushy plants, against which they can lean. Even for the most hard-working gardener it must be pleasant to have a plant that requires no attention.

Aconitum carmichaelii var. *wilsonii*
Aconitum napellus
Agastache—all species
Amsonia tabernaemontana var. *salicifolia*
Angelica gigas
Aruncus 'Horatio'
Aster lateriflorus 'Horizontalis'
Baptisia australis
Dendranthema 'Anja's Bouquet'
Dendranthema 'Herbstbrokat'
Dictamnus albus
Echinacea purpurea
Eupatorium maculatum 'Album'
Eupatorium maculatum 'Purple Bush'
Filipendula purpurea
Foeniculum vulgare
Gillenia trifoliata
Glycyrrhiza yunnanensis
Helenium—all species
Helianthus 'Lemon Queen'
Kalimeris incisa
Lavatera—all species
Liatris—all species
Lythrum virgatum
Miscanthus—all species
Monarda—all species

Nepeta latifolia
Panicum virgatum 'Cloud Nine'
Panicum virgatum 'Dallas Blues'
Persicaria polymorpha
Peucedanum verticillare
Phlomis tuberosa 'Amazone'
Phlox paniculata 'Lichtspel'
Salvia argentea
Salvia nemorosa
Salvia sclarea
Sanguisorba canadensis
Scutellaria incana

Sanguisorba canadensis

Sedum telephium 'Matrona'
Selinum wallichianum
Sidalcea—all species
Strobilanthus atropurpureus
Tanacetum macrophyllum
Thalictrum 'Elin'
Thalictrum polygamum
Thalictrum rochebruneanum
Verbascum lychnitis
Verbena hastata
Verbesina alternifolia

Imperialistic plants

Some plants have a tendency to keep on demanding more space for themselves, at the cost of their neighbors. They do this by being strongly rampant or by dropping their seeds in the centers of other plants. Such plants are totally unsuitable for lazy gardeners because, before you know what is happening, there will be only one species of plant in the garden. If you can keep everything under control, such invasive plants and profuse seeders can be fun because they give the garden a natural look. In the list that follows an R in front of the plant name means it is rampant, an S that it is a profuse self-seeder.

S *Artemisia absinthium*
R *Artemisia ludoviciana* var. *latiloba*
R + S *Aster umbellatus*
S *Brachypodium sylvaticum*
S *Briza media*
S *Calamagrostis brachytricha*

S *Carex grayi*
S *Carex pendula*
S *Cephalaria gigantea*
S *Deschampsia cespitosa*
S *Digitalis*—all species
S *Echinops sphaerocephalus*
R *Epilobium angustifolium*
S *Eragrostis curvula*
S *Eupatorium cannabinum* 'Album'
R *Euphorbia cyparissias* 'Fens Ruby'
R *Filipendula rubra* 'Venusta'
S *Foeniculum vulgare*
R *Geranium clarkei* 'Kashmir White'
R *Geranium macrorrhizum*
S *Geranium maculatum*
S *Geranium nodosum*
S *Geranium phaeum*
S *Geranium pratense*
R *Houttuynia cordata*
S *Knautia dipsacifolia*
S *Lamium orvala*
S *Linaria purpurea*
S *Lunaria rediviva*
R *Lysimachia ciliata*
R *Nepeta sibirica*
S *Origanum vulgare*
S *Pimpinella major* var. *rosea*
S *Salvia verticillata*
S *Smyrnium perfoliatum*
S *Succisella inflexa*
S *Thalictrum aquilegifolium*
S *Thalictrum delavayi*
S *Thalictrum flavum* subsp. *glaucum*
S *Thalictrum lucidum*
S *Verbascum lychnitis*
S *Verbena*—all species
S *Viola sororia*

Weavers and climbers

A small number of short plants are inclined to produce long, weak stalks that grow through and over neighboring plants. They all flower over a long period. Such plants should be planted together with early flowering species, which are ugly after flowering.

Borago pygmaea
Ceratostigma plumbaginoides
Clematis integrifolia
Geranium 'Ann Folkard'
Geranium 'Dilys'
Geranium soboliferum
Geranium wallichianum 'Buxton's Variety'
Potentilla xhopwoodiana
Potentilla 'Volcan'
Viola cornuta
Viola cornuta 'Alba'

Butterfly plants

Along with the growing interest in nature and natural gardening, interest in all that zooms and buzzes, which adds something special to the summer garden, has increased immensely. Here follows a list of the most important butterfly tempters among the plants named in this book. The best of all are marked with an asterisk.

Agastache rugosa
Asclepias incarnata
Aster—all species*
Astrantia major
Cephalaria—all species
Dianthus—all species
*Echinacea purpurea**
Echinops—all species
Eryngium—all species
Eupatorium—all species*
Helenium—all species

Knautia macedonica

Helianthus 'Lemon Queen'*
Knautia—all species
Leucanthemella serotina
Liatris—all species*
*Lunaria rediviva**
Lythrum virgatum
Monarda—all species*
Origanum laevigatum
*Origanum vulgare**
Persicaria amplexicaulis
Phlox paniculata
Pulmonaria—all species
Sanguisorba—all species
Scabiosa—all species*
*Sedum spectabile**
Silphium—all species
*Succisa pratensis**
*Succisella inflexa**
*Verbena bonariensis**
Verbena hastata
Vernonia crinita
Veronicastrum virginicum

Rabbit resistant

Rabbits can present a big problem for people who live in richly wooded areas. The best solution is to put up a fence of wire netting around the garden: 1 m above and 40 cm below the surface. If for some reason this is not feasible, then restrict the garden to plants that do not appeal to rabbits. The following list has been drawn up with some reservations. In practice, rabbits are rather fickle. Plants that they gorge on, down to the very last leaf, one year are ignored the next. True, plants that are poisonous are not eaten but sometimes they are bitten off at ground level or dug up. Nothing is truly rabbit proof.

Aconitum—all species
Actaea—all species
Alchemilla—all species
Amsonia—all species
Anemone—all species
Angelica—all species
Artemisia—all species
Aster—all species
Astilbe—all species
Baptisia—all species
Calamagrostis—all species
Calamintha—all species

Campanula lactiflora
Delphinium—all species
Dictamnus albus
Digitalis—all species
Epilobium angustifolium
Epimedium—all species
Eupatorium—all species
Euphorbia—all species
Gentiana—all species
Geranium—all species
Geum rivale
Gillenia trifoliata
Helleborus—all species
Hemerocallis—all species
Hosta—all species
Inula—all species
Iris—all species

Lamium—all species
Ligularia—all species
Lysimachia—all species
Miscanthus—all species
Molinia—all species
Monarda—all species
Nepeta—all species
Panicum virgatum
Papaver orientale
Persicaria—all species
Potentilla—all species
Pulmonaria—all species
Ranunculus—all species
Rodgersia—all species
Saponaria xlempergii 'Max Frei'
Scutellaria incana
Sedum—all species
Solidago—all species
Stachys—all species
Stipa—all species
Strobilanthes atropurpureus
Tricyrtis—all species
Veratrum—all species
Verbascum lychnitis
Veronica—all species
Veronicastrum virginicum

Coastal plants

Gardening close to the sea is not a sinecure. Gales, and especially the salt-laden winds that blow from the sea, form an insurmountable problem. In general, it is advisable to avoid tall and weak plants. Bushy plants perform better. Coastal inhabitants have one advantage: numerous plants, which are not hardy inland, thrive close to the sea.

Achillea hybrids
Achnatherum calamagrostis
Alchemilla—all species
Artemisia—gray-leaved species
Aster—low-growing species
Briza media
Calamagrostis xacutiflora
Centaurea—all species
Crambe maritima—obviously!
Dianthus—all species
Eragrostis—all species
Eryngium—all species
Euphorbia cyparissias
Festuca mairei
Geranium—all species
Glaucium corniculatum
Heuchera micrantha
Knautia—all species
Lavatera—all species
Limonium latifolium
Linaria purpurea
Mertensia virginica

Miscanthus—all species
Origanum—all species
Penstemon—all species
Perovskia abrotanoides
Petrorhagia saxifraga
Phlomis—all species
Salvia—short species
Saponaria xlempergii 'Max Frei'
Scabiosa—all species
Sedum—all species
Sesleria nitida
Stipa—all species

Sedum telephium subsp. *maximum* 'Atropurpureum'

Evergreen plants

In addition to all the beautiful winter silhouettes, evergreen perennials also contribute to an attractive winter garden. A disadvantage for many of the evergreens is that when a period of frost persists for more than a few days, at temperatures of below 10 degrees Celsius, they must be protected.

Asarum europaeum
Asphodeline lutea
Briza media
Carex grayi
Carex pendula
Deschampsia cespitosa
Digitalis ferruginea
Epimedium xperralchicum 'Frohnleiten'
Epimedium xversicolor 'Sulphureum'
Euphorbia amygdaloides var. *robbiae*
Geranium macrorrhizum
Glaucium corniculatum
Helleborus—all species
Iris foetidissima
Lamium maculatum—cultivars
Linaria purpurea
Oxalis acetosella
Papaver orientale
Ranunculus gramineus
Salvia officinalis 'Berggarten'

Actaea mairei

Plants per Square Meter

An often-repeated question is how many plants of each species should be planted in the garden. We have, therefore, compiled a list of all the genera that appear in this book and indicated how many plants are required per square meter. If you only wish to fill half that amount of space with one species, then naturally you only require half the number of plants. When a genus has more than one species, the number of plants per square meter may vary. The lowest number refers to the larger species, the highest to the smaller species. It is important to consider the qualities of neighboring species, so that the plants will not overrun each other.

Perennials

7	Achillea
9	Aconitum
7	Actaea
7	Agastache
3-5	Alcea
7-11	Alchemilla
7	Amsonia
7	Anemone (summer and autumn flowering)
11	Anemone (spring flowering)
7	Angelica
7	Anthemis
9	Aquilegia
1	Aralia
5-7	Artemisia
5	Aruncus
11	Asarum
7	Asclepias
7	Asphodeline
5-7	Aster
7	Astilbe
5	Astilboides
7	Astrantia
3-5	Baptisia
9	Borago
7-9	Calamintha
7	Campanula
9	Cardamine
7	Centaurea
5	Cephalaria
7	Cirsium
1-3	Clematis
7	Codonopsis
5	Coreopsis

1-5	Crambe
7	Darmera
3	Datisca
7	Delphinium
5	Dendranthema
9-11	Dianthus
5	Dictamnus
7	Digitalis
7-9	Echinacea
7	Echinops
7	Epilobium
9	Epimedium
7-9	Eryngium
3-5	Eupatorium
5-11	Euphorbia
3-7	Filipendula
7	Foeniculum
7	Galega
7	Gaura
5-7	Gentiana
7-9	Geranium
9	Geum
5	Gillenia
5	Glaucium
1	Glycyrrhiza
5	Gypsophila
7	Helenium
3-5	Helianthus
7-11	Helleborus
7	Hemerocallis
9	Heuchera
3-7	Hosta
7	Houttuynia
3-7	Inula
7	Iris
7	Kalimeris
7	Kirengeshoma
7	Knautia
7-9	Lamium

1	Lavatera
9	Liatris
5	Ligularia
7	Limonium
7	Linaria
7	Lindelofia
7	Lobelia
7	Lunaria
7	Lychnis
7	Lysimachia
7	Lythrum
7	Marrubium
9	Mertensia
7	Molopospermum
7	Monarda
7	Nepeta
9	Origanum
11	Oxalis
7	Papaver
7	Penstemon
5	Perovskia
1-9	Persicaria
9	Petalostemum
9	Petrorhagia
7	Peucedanum
7	Phlomis
9	Phlox (spring flowering)
7	Phlox (summer flowering)
7	Pimpinella
11	Platycodon
7	Podophyllum
7	Polemonium
7	Polygonatum
7	Potentilla
9	Pulmonaria

7-11	Ranunculus
7	Rodgersia
5-7	Rudbeckia
7	Ruellia
7	Salvia
1-7	Sanguisorba
7	Saponaria
9	Saxifraga
7-9	Scabiosa
7	Scutellaria
7	Sedum
7	Selinum
7	Serratula
7	Sidalcea
3	Silphium
7	Sisyrinchium
7	Smilacina
9	Smyrnium
5-7	Solidago
7	xSolidaster
7	Stachys
3	Strobilanthes
7	Stylophorum
7	Succisa
7	Succisella
7	Tanacetum
3-7	Thalictrum
3	Trachystemon
7	Tricyrtis
7	Trifolium
5	Veratrum
7	Verbascum
7	Verbena
5	Verbesina
3	Vernonia
7	Veronica
5-7	Veronicastrum
11	Viola
7	Zigadenus

Ornamental grasses

3-5	Achnatherum
5	Brachypodium
7	Briza
3	Calamagrostis
3-5	Carex
5-7	Chasmantium
3-5	Deschampsia
7	Diarrhena
3-7	Eragrostis
1	Festuca mairei
7	Hakonechloa
9	Imperata
7	Milium
1-3	Miscanthus
3-5	Molinia
1-5	Panicum
3	Pennisetum
7	Schizachyrium
5	Sesleria
3	Sorghastrum
5	Spodiopogon
5	Sporobolus
1-7	Stipa

Literature list

Aden, P. 1990. *The Hosta Book*. 2nd ed. Portland, Oregon: Timber Press.

Bailey, L. H. 1976. *Hortus Third: A Concise Dictionary of Plants Cultivated in the United States and Canada*. New York: MacMillan Publishing.

Brown, L. 1985. *Grasslands*. National Audubon Society Nature Guides. New York: Alfred A. Knopf.

Foerster, K. 1982. *Einzug der Gräser und Farne in die Gärten*. 6th ed. Melsungen, Germany: J. Neumann-Neudamm.

Gerritsen, H. 1993. *Spelen met de Natuur: De natuur als inspiratiebron voor de tuin*. Warnsveld, Netherlands: Terra.

Gerritsen, H., and P. Oudolf. 2000. *Dream Plants for the Natural Garden*. Portland, Oregon: Timber Press.

Hinkley, D. 1999. *The Explorer's Garden: Rare and Unusual Perennials*. Portland, Oregon: Timber Press.

Jelitto, L., and W. Schacht. 1990. *Hardy Herbaceous Perennials*. 2 vols. 3rd ed. Portland, Oregon: Timber Press.

King, M., and P. Oudolf. 1998. *Gardening with Grasses*. Portland, Oregon: Timber Press.

Meijden, R. van der. 1996. *Heukels' Flora van Nederland*. 22nd ed. Groningen, Netherlands: Wolters-Noordhoff.

Ohwi, J. 1984. *Flora of Japan*. 2nd ed. Washington, D.C.: Smithsonian Institution Press.

Oudolf, P., and N. Kingsbury. 1999. *Designing with Plants*. Portland, Oregon: Timber Press.

Polunin, O. 1980. *Flowers of Greece and the Balkans: A Field Guide*. Oxford: Oxford University Press.

Polunin, O., and A. Stainton. 1985. *Flowers of the Himalaya*. Oxford: Oxford University Press.

Polunin, O., and B. E. Smythies. 1973. *Flowers of Southwest Europe: A Field Guide*. Oxford: Oxford University Press.

Royal Horticultural Society. 2002. *RHS Plant Finder 2003-2004*. London: Dorling Kindersley.

Thomas, G. S. 1990. *Perennial Garden Plants: Or the Modern Florilegium*. 3rd ed. Portland, Oregon: Timber Press.

Tutin, T., G., et al., eds. 1964-1980. *Flora Europaea*. Vols. 1-5. Cambridge: Cambridge University Press.

Nurseries and gardens

Canada

Free Spirit Nursery
20405 32 Avenue
Langley, BC V2Z 2C7
tel: (604) 533-7373

Netherlands

Oudolf nursery
Broekstraat 17
6999 DE Hummelo
tel: 314 381120
www.oudolf.com

Priona gardens (Henk Gerritsen)
Schuineslootweg 13
7777 RE Schuinesloot
tel: 523 681734
www.prionatuinen.com

United Kingdom

Four Seasons
Forncett St. Mary, Norwich NR16 1JT
tel: 1508 488344 (mail order)
www.fsperennials.co.uk

Marchant Hardy Plants (Graham Gough)
Ripe Road, Laughton
East Sussex BN8 6AJ
tel: 1323 811737 (retail)

Monksilver Nursery
Oakington Road, Cottenham
Cambridgeshire CB4 8TW
tel: 1954 251555 (mail order)
www.monksilver.com

Orchard Dene Nurseries
Lower Assendon, Henley on Thames
Oxfordshire RG9 1GA
tel: 1491 575075 (wholesale only)

United States

Earthly Pursuits
2901 Kuntz Rd., Windsor Mill, MD 21244
tel: 410 496 2523
www.earthlypursuits.com

Heronswood Nursery
7530 NE 288th St., Kingston, WA 98346
tel: 360 297 4172
www.heronswood.com

Northwind Perennial Farm
7047 Hospital Rd., Burlington, WI 53176
tel: 262 248 8229
www.northwindperennialfarm.com

Roslyn Nursery
211 Burrs Lane, Dix Hills, NY 11746
tel: 613 643 9347
www.roslynnursery.com

Photographic Acknowledgments

Piet Oudolf
Cover, page 6, 8, 12 above and left, 13, 16 left, center and below, 17 above, 20 above right, 21 above, 24 above, 25 above and left, 28, 29, 32, 36, 37 center left, 40 center and below left, 41, 44, 45, 48 center right and below right, 49 center and below, 52 above, center right and below, 53 above, center and below left, 56 above, center left and below left, 57 center and below, 60, 61 below left, 64 center, 64/65 above, 65, 68, 69 above and below right, 72, 73, 76, 78, 79, 82 above right and center, 83, 86, 87, 88, 93, 94, 95, 96, 98, 99, 117, 118, 119, 100/101, 102/103, 104/105, 108/109, 110, 114, 121, 122, 123, 124, 126, 127, 132, 133, 134, 135 left, 136.

Anton Schlepers
Page 12 right, 16 above, 17 below, 20 above left, 21 below, 24 center left and below, 25 below right, 33, 37 above and below right, 40 above and below right, 48 above en below left, 49 above, 52 center left, 53 below right, 56 below right, 57 above right, 61 above right, 64 above left and below, 69 center left, 82 above left and below left, 90, 91, 92, 106, 107, 111, 112, 115, 120, 137 right.

Henk Gerritsen
Page 20 below, 24 center right, 84, 100.

Index of Plant Names

Boldfaced numbers indicate pages with photos.

Achillea 10, 67, 90, 132, 135
Achillea 'Credo' 10, 103
Achillea 'Hella Glashoff' 10, **12**, 103, 126, 128, **133**
Achillea 'Lilac Beauty' 10, 129
Achillea millefolium 10
Achillea 'Schwefelblüte' 10
Achillea 'Summerwine' 10, 107, 123, 127, 129
Achillea 'Walther Funcke' 10, 106, 110, 126, 129
Achillea 'Wesersandstein' 10, **52**
Achnatherum 76
Achnatherum calamagrostis 76, 90, **115**, 135
Aconitum 10, 67, 94, 135
Aconitum carmichaelii var. wilsonii 10, **78**, 122, 129, 133
Aconitum episcopale 10, 122
Aconitum lamarckii 10, **115**, 128, 133
Aconitum napellus 10, 129, 133
Aconitum napellus 'Grandiflorum Album' 10
Aconitum napellus 'Pink Sensation' 10, **12**
Aconitum napellus 'Stainless Steel' 10, **132**
Aconitum septentrionale 'Ivorine' 10
Actaea 10, 94, 135
Actaea cordifolia 10, 122
Actaea heracleifolia 10
Actaea japonica 11, 122
Actaea mairei 11, 122, **135**
Actaea matsumurae 122
Actaea pachypoda 10, 128
Actaea rubra 10
Actaea rubra 'Neglecta' 10
Actaea rubra f. neglecta 10
Actaea simplex 98, 122
Actaea simplex var. matsumurae 'White Pearl' 11
Actaea simplex var. simplex 'Atropurpurea' 11
Actaea simplex var. simplex 'James Compton' 11, **96**, 127, 128
Actaea simplex var. simplex 'Prichard's Giant' 11
Actaea simplex var. simplex 'Scimitar' 11, **12**, 129
Actaea spicata 10
Agastache 11, 90, 119, 123, 132, 134, 133
Agastache nepetoides 11
Agastache rugosa 11, 103, 127, 129
Agastache rugosa 'Alabaster' 11
Agastache rugosa 'Blue Fortune' 11, 126, 129
Alcea 10, 90, 123, 132, 134
Alcea ficifolia 11
Alcea rosea 'Nigra' 11, **12**, 103
Alcea rugosa 11
Alchemilla 11, 135
Alchemilla conjuncta 11, 110, 129
Alchemilla erythropoda 11, **12**, 128
Alexanders, see Smyrnium
Althaea 11
Althaea 'Parkallee' 11, **99**
Amsonia 11, 135

Amsonia hubrichtii 11, **49**, 118, 127, 129
Amsonia orientalis 14, 90, 128
Amsonia tabernaemontana var. salicifolia 14, **16**, 103, 118, 126, 128, 133
Anemone 14, 135
Anemone cylindrica 14, **16**, 110, 128
Anemone hupehensis 14, 94, 122
Anemone hupehensis 'Crispa' 14
Anemone hupehensis 'Hadspen Abundance' 14
Anemone xhybrida 14, 94, 122
Anemone xhybrida 'Honorine Jobert' 14, **20**, 127, 129
Anemone xhybrida 'Königin Charlotte' 14
Anemone xhybrida 'Lady Gilmour', see A. hupehensis 'Crispa'
Anemone xhybrida 'Pamina' 14
Anemone xhybrida 'Whirlwind' 14
Anemone xlesseri 14
Anemone leveillei 14, 94, 128
Anemone multifida 14
Anemone sylvestris 14, 90, 128
Anemone sylvestris 'Macrantha' 14
Anemone tomentosa 14, 94, 122
Anemone tomentosa 'Albadura' 14, 128
Anemone tomentosa 'Robustissima' 14, **16**, 127
Angelica 14, 132, 134, 135
Angelica gigas 14, **126**, 133
Angelica sylvestris 'Vicar's Mead' 14, 110
aniseed, see Pimpinella anisum
Anthemis 14
Anthemis xhybrida 'E. C. Buxton' 14, 90, 123, 129, 132, 134
Aquilegia 15, 132, 134
Aquilegia akitensis, see A. flabellata
Aquilegia flabellata 15, 128
Aquilegia xhybrida 'Nora Barlow' 15, **17**
Aralia 15, 94
Aralia californica 15, 133
Aralia continentalis 15
Aralia racemosa 15
Artemisia 15, 90, 110, 135
Artemisia absinthium 15, 134
Artemisia absinthium 'Lambrook Silver' 15
Artemisia alba 'Canescens' 15
Artemisia lactiflora 15, 94, 122
Artemisia lactiflora Guizhou Group 'Rosa Schleier' 15, **16**, **24**, 98
Artemisia ludoviciana var. latiloba 15, 133, 134
Aruncus 15, 19
Aruncus 'Horatio' 15, **17**, 94, 98, 118, 119, 133
Asarum 15, 94
Asarum canadense 15
Asarum europaeum 18
Asclepias 18
Asclepias 'Alba' 18
Asclepias incarnata 18, 103, **118**, 127, 129, 134
Asperella 76
Asperella hystrix 76

Asphodeline 18
Asphodeline lutea 18, **20**, 90, 110, 128, 135
Aster 18, 66, 122, 134, 135
Aster amellus 18, 123
Aster amellus 'Rosa Erfüllung' 18, **20**
Aster amellus 'Sonora' 18, 127
Aster 'Anja's Choice' 18
Aster cordifolius 18, 122
Aster cordifolius 'Little Carlow' 18, 129
Aster divaricatus 18, 123, 133
Aster ericoides 18, 122
Aster ericoides 'Blue Star' 18
Aster xfrikartii 'Mönch' 18, 123, 129, 133
Aster 'Herfstweelde' 18
Aster laevis 18, 122
Aster lateriflorus 122
Aster lateriflorus 'Horizontalis' 18, 119, 129, 133
Aster macrophyllus 18
Aster macrophyllus 'Twilight' 18, 123, 126, 128, 133
Aster novae-angliae 18, 122
Aster novae-angliae 'Andenken an Alma Pötschke' 18
Aster novae-angliae 'Septemberrubin' 18
Aster novae-angliae 'Violetta' 18, **20**, 127, 129
Aster 'Oktoberlicht' 18
Aster umbellatus 18, **87**, 119, 122, 128, 133, 134
Astilbe 18, 94, 119, 135
Astilbe chinensis var. taquetii 'Purpurlanze' 19, 106, 126, 128, 129
Astilbe simplicifolia 19
Astilbe simplicifolia 'Dunkellachs' 19
Astilbe simplicifolia 'Sprite' 19
Astilbe thunbergii 'Prof. van der Wielen' 19
Astilboides 19
Astilboides tabularis 19, 94
Astrantia 19, 94
Astrantia major 19, 128, 134, 134
Astrantia major 'Claret' 19, 106, 126, 129
Astrantia major 'Roma' 19, **87**, 126, 127, 128
Astrantia major 'Washfield' 19
Astrantia major subsp. involucrata 19
Astrantia major subsp. involucrata 'Canneman' 19, **21**
Astrantia major subsp. involucrata 'Margery Fish', see A. major subsp. involucrata 'Shaggy'
Astrantia major subsp. involucrata 'Shaggy' 19
Astrantia maxima 19, **21**
Atriplex hortensis var. rubra **111**
avens, see Geum

baby's breath, see Gypsophila
balloon flower, see Platycodon
baneberry, see Actaea
Baptisia 19, 135
Baptisia australis 19, 90, **90**, 118, 128, 129, 133

Baptisia lactea 19
Baptisia 'Purple Smoke' 19
barrenwort, see Epimedium
bellflower, see Campanula
bergamot, see Monarda
bishop's hat, see Epimedium
blue grass, see Sesleria
borage, see Borago
Borago 19
Borago laxiflora, see B. pygmaea
Borago pygmaea 19, 90, 123, 132, 134, 134
bottlebrush grass, see Asperella
Brachypodium 76
Brachypodium sylvaticum 76, 98, 129, 132, 134
Briza 76
Briza media 76, 134, 135
Briza media 'Limouzi' 76, 126, 129
burnet, see Sanguisorba
burnet saxifrage, see Pimpinella
burning bush, see Dictamnus
butter bur, see Petasites hybridus
buttercup, see Ranunculus

Calamagrostis 76, 135
Calamagrostis xacutiflora 76, 135
Calamagrostis xacutiflora 'Karl Foerster' 76, 119, 126, 129, 133
Calamagrostis xacutiflora 'Overdam' 76
Calamagrostis brachytricha 76, **115**, 118, 122, 129, 134
calamint, see Calamintha
Calamintha 19, 135
Calamintha grandiflora 19
Calamintha nepeta subsp. nepeta 22, 90, 122, 128
Calamintha nepeta subsp. nepeta 'Alba' 22
Calamintha nepetoides, see C. nepeta subsp. nepeta
Camassia leichtlinii **95**
Campanula 22, 23, 67
Campanula 'Burghaltii' 22, **24**, 129, 133
Campanula 'Kent Belle' 22, 133
Campanula lactiflora 22, **24**, **73**, 94, 129, 135
Campanula lactiflora 'Loddon Anna' 22
Campanula latiloba 22
Campanula latiloba 'Alba' 22
Campanula latiloba 'Hidcote Amethyst' 22
Campanula 'Sarastro' 22
cap plant, see Silphium
Cardamine 22
Cardamine waldsteinii 22, 94
Carex 77, 94
Carex elata 'Aurea' 77
Carex grayi 77, 128, 134, 135
Carex muskingumensis 77, 128, 129
Carex pendula 77, 86, 133, 134, 135
Carex stricta 'Aurea', see C. elata 'Aurea'
carnation, see Dianthus
Carthusian pink, see Dianthus carthusianorum
catmint, see Nepeta

celandine, see *Chelidonium majus*
Centaurea 22, 135
Centaurea benoistii 22, 90
Centaurea glastifolia 22, **24**, 90, 128
Centaurea montana 22, 94
Centaurea montana 'Carnea' 22, 128
Centaurea 'Pulchra Major' 22, 90, 110
Cephalaria 22, 98, 134
Cephalaria alpina 'Nana' 22
Cephalaria dipsacoides 22
Cephalaria gigantea 22, **24**, 94, 133, 134
Ceratostigma 22
Ceratostigma plumbaginoides 22, 118, 122, 134
Chasmantium 77
Chasmantium latifolium 77, **78**, 122, 129
chamomile, see *Anthemis*
Chelidonium majus 66
Chrysopogon, see *Sorghastrum*
cinquefoil, see *Potentilla*
Cirsium 23
Cirsium rivulare 'Atropurpureum' 23, **25**, 94, 123, 128
Clematis 23, 94
Clematis heracleifolia 'China Purple' 23, 122
Clematis integrifolia 23, **25**, 133, 134
Clematis integrifolia 'Alba' 23
Clematis integrifolia 'Rosea' 23
Clematis xjouiniana 122, 133
Clematis xjouiniana 'Mrs Robert Brydon' 23
Clematis xjouiniana 'Praecox' 23
Clematis recta 23, 133
Clematis recta 'Purpurea' 23
clover, see *Trifolium*
coat flower, see *Petrorhagia*
Codonopsis 23
Codonopsis clematidea 23
columbine, see *Aquilegia*
common agrimony, see *Eupatorium*
cone flower, see *Echinacea*
coral flower, see *Heuchera*
Coreopsis 23
Coreopsis tripteris 23, **25**, 122, 129
Crambe cordifolia 23, **57**, 98, 129
Crambe maritima 23, 90, 110, **111**, 135
cranesbill, see *Geranium*

Dalea, see *Petalostemum*
Darmera 23
Darmera peltata 15, 23, 94, **95**, **116**, 118, 133
Datisca 26
Datisca cannabina 26, 90, 123, **126**, 129
day lily, see *Hemerocallis*
dead nettle, see *Lamium*
Delphinium 26, 133, 135
Delphinium 'Astolat' 26
Delphinium xbelladonna 'Casa Blanca' 26
Delphinium xbelladonna 'Cliveden Beauty' 26
Delphinium 'Berghimmel' 26
Delphinium 'Black Knight' 26
Delphinium 'Cameliard' 26
Delphinium elatum 26, 106, 126, 128
Delphinium 'Galahad' 26
Delphinium 'Lanzenträger' 26

Delphinium 'Zauberflöte' 26
Dendranthema 26, 122
Dendranthema 'Anja's Bouquet' 26, 133
Dendranthema 'Herbstbrokat' 26, **28**, 133
Dendranthema 'Paul Boissier' 26, **28**
Deschampsia 77
Deschampsia cespitosa 27, **76**, 77, 94, 98, 119, 128, 133, 134, 135
Deschampsia cespitosa 'Goldschleier' 77, **107**
Deschampsia cespitosa 'Goldtau' 77, 106, 126
devil's bit scabious, see *Succisa*
Dianthus 26, 90, 134, 135
Dianthus amurensis 26, 123
Dianthus carthusianorum 26, **49**, 127, 128
Dianthus sanguineus 26, **28**
Diarrhena 77
Diarrhena japonica 77, 98
Dictamnus 26
Dictamnus albus 26, 90, 129, 133, 135
Dictamnus albus 'Albiflorus' 26, **90**
Digitalis 26, 132, 134, 135
Digitalis ambigua, see *D. grandiflora*
Digitalis ferruginea 26, 106, 119, 126, 128, 135
Digitalis grandiflora 27, 128
Digitalis lutea 27
Digitalis xmertonensis 27
Digitalis parviflora 27, **29**, 119, 126, 129
Dracocephalum sibiricum, see *Nepeta sibirica*

Echinacea 27, 123
Echinacea pallida 27, 126, 129
Echinacea paradoxa 27, **49**, 119, 129
Echinacea purpurea 27, 133, 134
Echinacea purpurea 'Augustkönigin' 27
Echinacea purpurea 'Green Edge' 27
Echinacea purpurea 'Jade' 27, **29**
Echinacea purpurea 'Magnus' 27
Echinacea purpurea 'Rubinglow' 27, 106, **126**, 127
Echinacea purpurea 'Rubinstern' 27, 106
Echinacea purpurea 'Vintage Wine' 27
Echinacea purpurea 'White Lustre' 27
Echinops 27, 134
Echinops bannaticus 27
Echinops exaltatus 27
Echinops ritro 'Veitch's Blue' 27
Echinops sphaerocephalus 27, **29**, 133, 134
Echium 27
Echium russicum 27, 90, 132, 134
Epilobium 27
Epilobium angustifolium 27, 90, 118, 134, 135
Epilobium angustifolium 'Album' 27
Epilobium angustifolium 'Stahl Rose' 27, **29**
Epimedium 27, 135
Epimedium grandiflorum 30
Epimedium grandiflorum 'Lilac Seedling' 30, **33**
Epimedium macranthum, see *E. grandiflorum*
Epimedium xperralchicum 'Frohnleiten' 30, 135

Epimedium xrubrum 30
Epimedium xversicolor 'Sulphureum' 30, 129, 135
Epimedium xyoungianum 30
Epimedium xyoungianum 'Niveum' 30
Epimedium xyoungianum 'Roseum' 30
Eragrostis 77, 90, 98, 135
Eragrostis curvula 77, **127**, 134
Eragrostis spectabilis 77, **78**, 122
Eragrostis trichodes 77, 122
Eryngium 30, 90, 119, 134, 135
Eryngium alpinum 30
Eryngium bourgatii 30, **87**, 103, 129
Eryngium giganteum 30, **45**, **87**, **88**, **108-109**, 110, 126, 128, 132, 134
Eryngium xtripartitum 30, **33**
Eryngium yuccifolium 30, 110, 127, 129
Eupatorium 30, 94, 119, 122, 133, 134, 135
Eupatorium cannabinum 30
Eupatorium cannabinum 'Album' 30, 134
Eupatorium cannabinum 'Plenum' 30
Eupatorium maculatum 30, 118
Eupatorium maculatum 'Album' 30, 133
Eupatorium maculatum 'Atropurpureum' 30, **33**, **87**, **118**, 127-129
Eupatorium maculatum 'Purple Bush' 30, 127, 133
Eupatorium purpureum 'Album' 129
Eupatorium rugosum 30, 129
Eupatorium rugosum 'Chocolate' 30
Eupatorium rugosum 'Snowball' 31
Euphorbia 31, 135
Euphorbia amygdaloides var. *robbiae* 31, 135
Euphorbia corallioides 31, 129, 132, 134
Euphorbia cyparissias 118, 135
Euphorbia cyparissias 'Fens Ruby' 31, 90, 134
Euphorbia griffithii 'Dixter' 31, 94, 106, 127, 128, 133
Euphorbia palustris 31, **94**, **116**, 118, 133
Euphorbia robbiae, see *E. amygdaloides* var. *robbiae*
Euphorbia sarawschanica 31
Euphorbia schillingii 31, 118, 123

false hellebore, see *Veratrum*
false indigo, see *Baptisia*
false Solomon's seal, see *Smilacina*
feather grass, see *Stipa*
fennel, see *Foeniculum*
fescue, see *Festuca*
Festuca 77
Festuca mairei 77, 90, 98, 135
Filipendula 31, 94, 119
Filipendula kamtschatica 31, 133
Filipendula purpurea 31, 128, 133
Filipendula purpurea 'Alba' 31
Filipendula purpurea 'Elegans' 31
Filipendula purpurea 'Nephele' 31, 103
Filipendula rubra 'Venusta' 31, **33**, **100**, 126, 129
Filipendula rubra 'Venusta Magnifica' 86, 133, 134
fleabane, see *Inula*
florist's anemone, see *Anemone coronaria*

foam flower, see *Tiarella*
Foeniculum 31
Foeniculum vulgare 31, 90, 98, 119, 123, 132, 133, 134
Foeniculum vulgare 'Giant Bronze' 31, **87**, **99**, 103, **112**, 126
fountain grass, see *Pennisetum*
foxglove, see *Digitalis*

Galega 31
Galega orientalis 31, 128
Gaura 31
Gaura lindheimeri 31, 118, 123, 132, 134
Gaura lindheimeri 'Siskiyou Pink' 31
Gaura lindheimeri 'Whirling Butterflies' 31, 103, 128
gentian, see *Gentiana*
Gentiana 34, 135
Gentiana asclepiadea **33**, 34, 67, 94, 122
Gentiana asclepiadea 'Alba' 34
Gentiana lutea 34
Geranium 34, 135
Geranium 'Ann Folkard' 35, 94, 134
Geranium armenum, see *G. psilostemon*
Geranium 'Brookside' 35
Geranium xcantabrigiense 34
Geranium xcantabrigiense 'Biokovo' 34
Geranium xcantabrigiense 'Cambridge' 34
Geranium clarkei 'Kashmir Pink' 34
Geranium clarkei 'Kashmir Purple' 34
Geranium clarkei 'Kashmir White' 34, 134
Geranium 'Dilys' 35, 123, 134
Geranium macrorrhizum 34, 94, 133, 134, 135
Geranium macrorrhizum 'Album' 34, 129
Geranium macrorrhizum 'Czakor' 34
Geranium maculatum 34, 94, 128, 134
Geranium nodosum 34, 123, 128, 133, 134
Geranium nodosum 'Whiteleaf' 34, **36**
Geranium xoxonianum 34, 94, 123, 128, 129
Geranium xoxonianum 'Rebecca Moss' 34
Geranium xoxonianum 'Rose Clair' 34, 126
Geranium xoxonianum 'Sherwood' 34
Geranium xoxonianum 'Thurstonianum' 34, **36**
Geranium xoxonianum 'Wageningen' 34
Geranium palustre 34, 94
Geranium phaeum 34, **37**, 94, 133, 134
Geranium phaeum 'Album' 34
Geranium phaeum 'Calligrapher' 34
Geranium phaeum 'Lily Lovell' 34, 129
Geranium phaeum 'Rose Madder' 34
Geranium phaeum 'Samobor' 34
Geranium phaeum 'Springtime' 34, 128
Geranium pratense **25**, 34, 133, 134
Geranium pratense 'Mrs Kendall Clark' 35
Geranium pratense 'Silver Queen' 35
Geranium pratense 'Victor Reiter' 35
Geranium pratense 'White Lady' 35
Geranium psilostemon 35, **36**, 94, 106, 126, 128, 129
Geranium renardii 35, 110
Geranium renardii 'Philippe Vapelle' 35
Geranium sanguineum 35, 90
Geranium sanguineum 'Album' 35

Geranium sanguineum 'Ankum's Pride' 35
Geranium sanguineum 'Khan' 35
Geranium sanguineum var. striatum 35
Geranium 'Sirak' 35
Geranium soboliferum 35, 118, 123, 127, 129, 134
Geranium 'Spinners' 35
Geranium sylvaticum 94
Geranium sylvaticum 'Amy Doncaster' 35, 36, 128, 133
Geranium versicolor 34
Geranium wallichianum 'Buxton's Variety' 35, 123, 134
Geranium wlassovianum 35, 118, 123, 129
germander, see Teucrium
Geum 35
Geum rivale 35, 94, 135
Geum rivale 'Beech House Apricot' 35
Geum rivale 'Leonard' 35, 37, 86, 126, 128
giant hyssop, see Agastache
Gillenia 35
Gillenia trifoliata 35, 37, 118, 126, 128, 133, 135
Glaucium 35
Glaucium corniculatum 35, 45, 90, 110, 123, 132, 134, 135
globe thistle, see Echinops
Glycyrrhiza 38
Glycyrrhiza yunnanensis 38, 41, 119, 122, 133
goat's beard, see Aruncus
goat's rue, see Galega
golden beard grass, see Sorghastrum
golden rod, see Solidago
Gypsophila 38
Gypsophila altissima 38, 90, 98, 133

hair grass, see Deschampsia
Hakonechloa 77
Hakonechloa macra 76, 77, 118, 129
Hakonechloa macra 'Aureola' 77
heartsease, see Viola cornuta
Helenium 38, 122, 133, 134
Helenium autumnale 'Die Blonde' 38, 106
Helenium 'Flammendes Käthchen' 38
Helenium 'Kupferzwerg' 38, 40,106, 126
Helenium 'Rubinkuppel' 38, 41, 129
Helenium 'Rubinzwerg' 33, 38, 127
Helenium 'Zimbelstern' 38
Helianthus 38, 122, 133
Helianthus 'Lemon Queen' 20, 38, 133, 134
Helianthus salicifolius 38, 41
hellebore, see Helleborus
Helleborus 38, 94, 135
Helleborus argutifolius 38
Helleborus atrorubens 38
Helleborus foetidus 38, 132, 134
Helleborus lividus subsp. corsicus, see H. argutifolius
Helleborus odorus 39, 41, 129
Helleborus orientalis 'Early Purple' 39
Helleborus orientalis 'Party Dress' 39
Helleborus orientalis Picotees 39
Helleborus orientalis Westwood hybrids 39
Helleborus purpurascens 39
Hemerocallis 39, 118, 133, 135

Hemerocallis altissima 39
Hemerocallis citrina 39
Hemerocallis citrina x H. ochroleuca 39
Hemerocallis 'Corky' 39
Hemerocallis 'Gentle Shepherd' 39
Hemerocallis 'Green Flutter' 39, 126, 127
Hemerocallis 'Joan Senior' 39, 127
Hemerocallis 'Little Grapette' 39
Hemerocallis 'Nugget' 39, 41, 106
Hemerocallis 'Pardon Me' 39, 106
Hemerocallis 'Princess Blue Eyes' 39, 41
Hemerocallis 'Uri Winniford' 39
herb Christopher, see Actaea
Heuchera 39
Heuchera micrantha 94, 128, 135
Heuchera micrantha 'Palace Purple' 39, 41, 128
hog's fennel, see Peucedanum
hogweed, see Heracleum
hollyhock, see Alcea
honesty, see Lunaria
horehound, see Marrubium
horned poppy, see Glaucium
Hosta 39, 94, 118, 119, 133, 135
Hosta 'Blue Angel' 42, 110, 129
Hosta 'Blue Impression' 42, 110, 126
Hosta clausa 39
Hosta clausa var. normalis 39
Hosta 'Krossa Regal' 42, 110
Hosta 'Midas Touch' 42
Hosta plantaginea 'Grandiflora' 122
Hosta plantaginea var. grandiflora 39
Hosta sieboldiana 39
Hosta sieboldiana 'Elegans' 39, 110, 128
Hosta sieboldiana var. fortunei 'Hadspen Blue', see H. tokudama 'Hadspen Blue'
Hosta sieboldiana 'Frances Williams' 42, 129
Hosta 'Sum and Substance' 42
Hosta xtardiana 42
Hosta xtardiana 'Blue Moon' 42, 110
Hosta xtardiana 'Halcyon' 42, 45, 110, 126
Hosta tokudama 'Hadspen Blue' 42, 110, 128
Hosta ventricosa 'Aureomarginata' 42
Hosta 'White Triumphator' 42
Houttuynia 42
Houttuynia cordata 42, 94, 134
Hystrix patula, see Asperella hystrix

Imperata 77
Imperata cylindrica 'Red Baron' 77, 78
Inula 42, 135
Inula hookeri 42, 94
Inula magnifica 42, 90, 133
Inula magnifica 'Sonnenstrahl' 16, 42
Iris 42, 94, 135
Iris chrysographes 42
Iris foetidissima 42, 135

Jacob's ladder, see Polemonium
Jacob's rod, see Asphodeline
Japanese anemone 14
Japanese bloodgrass, see Imperata
Japanese waxflower, see Kirengeshoma
Joe Pye weed, see Eupatorium maculatum

Kalimeris 42
Kalimeris incisa 42, 123, 128, 129, 133
Kalimeris incisa 'Alba' 42
Kalimeris pinnatifida 'Hortensis' 42, 122
Kirengeshoma 43
Kirengeshoma palmata 43, 94, 119, 122, 128
knapweed, see Centaurea
Knautia 43, 134, 135
Knautia dipsacifolia 43, 126, 129, 133, 134
Knautia drymeia 43
Knautia macedonica 43, 45, 90, 133, 134
knotweed, see Persicaria 51

lady's mantle, see Alchemilla
Lamium 43, 135
Lamium maculatum 43, 123, 135
Lamium maculatum 'Pink Pewter' 43
Lamium maculatum 'White Nancy' 43, 110
Lamium orvala 43, 94, 128, 129, 133, 134
Lamium orvala 'Album' 43, 45
Lavatera 43, 123, 133, 135
Lavatera cachemiriana 43, 57, 76, 129
Lavatera cachemiriana 'White Angel' 43, 127
Lavatera cachemiriana x L. thuringiaca 43
Lavatera cachemiriana x L. thuringiaca 'Summer Kisses' 43
Lavatera cachemiriana x L. thuringiaca 'Sweet Dream' 43
Lavatera cachemiriana x L. thuringiaca 'White Satin' 43, 45
lesser periwinkle, see Vinca minor
Leucanthemella 43
Leucanthemella serotina 43, 94, 122, 127, 129, 134
Liatris 43, 119, 133, 134
Liatris aspera 43, 106
Liatris ligulistylis 43, 45, 127
Liatris pycnostachya 43
Liatris spicata 43, 46
Liatris spicata 'Alba' 46, 128
licorice, see Glycyrrhiza
Ligularia 46, 94, 119, 135
Ligularia japonica 46
Ligularia macrophylla 46
Ligularia veitchiana 46, 123
Limonium 46
Limonium latifolium 46, 49, 88, 90, 98, 103, 118, 119, 126, 127, 128, 135
Linaria 46
Linaria purpurea 46, 98, 110, 123, 127, 132, 134, 135
Linaria purpurea 'Canon J. Went' 46
Linaria purpurea 'Springside White' 46, 49
Lindelofia 46
Lindelofia anchusoides 46, 49, 128
Lobelia 46, 94, 126, 132, 134
Lobelia cardinalis 46
Lobelia xgerardii 46
Lobelia xgerardii 'Eulalia Berridge' 46, 49
Lobelia xgerardii 'Vedrariensis' 46, 106, 129
Lobelia siphilitica 46, 129
Lobelia siphilitica 'Alba' 46
loosestrife, see Lysimachia, Lythrum
love grass, see Eragrostis
Lunaria 46

Lunaria rediviva 46, 92, 94, 95, 119, 128, 129, 133, 134
lungwort, see Pulmonaria
Lychnis 46
Lychnis chalcedonica 46
Lychnis chalcedonica 'Alba' 46, 49
Lychnis chalcedonica 'Carnea' 46, 128, 129
Lysimachia 47, 135
Lysimachia ciliata 47, 94, 134
Lysimachia ciliata 'Alexander' 47
Lysimachia ciliata 'Firecracker' 47
Lysimachia ephemerum 47, 49, 110, 123, 129
Lythrum 47, 94
Lythrum salicaria 47
Lythrum salicaria 'Blush' 47, 49
Lythrum salicaria 'Zigeunerblut' 47
Lythrum virgatum 47, 76, 119, 133, 134

mallow, see Althaea, Malva
marguerite, see Leucanthemella
marjoram, see Origanum
Marrubium 47
Marrubium incanum 47, 90, 110, 119
masterwort, see Astrantia
may apple, see Podophyllum
meadow cress, see Cardamine
meadow rue, see Thalictrum
meadow sweet, see Filipendula
Melica nutans 60
Mertensia 47
Mertensia sibirica 47, 128
Mertensia virginica 47, 49, 135
milfoil, see Achillea millefolium
Milium 77
Milium effusum 98
Milium effusum 'Aureum' 77, 94, 129
milk weed, see Asclepias
millet, see Milium, Panicum
Miscanthus 80, 118, 119, 122, 128, 133, 135
Miscanthus sinensis 80
Miscanthus sinensis 'Ferner Osten' 80
Miscanthus sinensis 'Flamingo' 80
Miscanthus sinensis 'Gewitterwolke' 80
Miscanthus sinensis 'Ghana' 80
Miscanthus sinensis 'Graziella' 80
Miscanthus sinensis 'Haiku' 80
Miscanthus sinensis 'Hermann Müssel' 80
Miscanthus sinensis 'Kaskade' 80
Miscanthus sinensis 'Kleine Fontäne' 80
Miscanthus sinensis 'Kleine Silberspinne' 80, 129
Miscanthus sinensis 'Krater' 80
Miscanthus sinensis 'Malepartus' 80, 87, 128, 129
Miscanthus sinensis 'Morning Light' 78, 80
Miscanthus sinensis 'Silberturm' 78
Miscanthus sinensis 'Undine' 80
Miscanthus sinensis 'Yakushima Dwarf' 80
Miscanthus sinensis 'Zwergelefant' 78, 80, 126
Molinia 80, 118, 122, 133, 135
Molinia altissima, see M. caerulea var. arundinacea
Molinia caerulea 80, 119
Molinia caerulea var. arundinacea 80
Molinia caerulea var. arundinacea

'Cordoba' 80
Molinia caerulea var. arundinacea 'Fontäne' 80
Molinia caerulea var. arundinacea 'Karl Foerster' 80, 127, 129
Molinia caerulea var. arundinacea 'Transparent' 80, 98, **118**, **120**, 126, **126**, 127, 129
Molinia caerulea var. arundinacea 'Windsäule' **78**, 80
Molinia caerulea 'Edith Dudszus' 80
Molinia caerulea 'Heidebraut' 80
Molinia caerulea 'Moorflamme' 80
Molinia caerulea 'Moorhexe' **78**, 80, 129
Molinia caerulea 'Poul Petersen' 80, 127
Molinia litoralis, see M. caerulea var. arundinacea
Molopospermum 47
Molopospermum peloponnesiacum 47, 126
Monarda 47, 119, **124**, 133, 134, 135
Monarda 'Aquarius' 47
Monarda 'Balance' 47
Monarda 'Beauty of Cobham' 47
Monarda 'Beauty of Livermore' 51
Monarda 'Cherokee' 47, 129
Monarda 'Elsie's Lavender' 47
Monarda 'Fishes' 47, 127
Monarda 'Flamingo' 51
Monarda 'Gardenview Scarlet' 50, 106
Monarda 'Juliane' 51
Monarda 'Karine' 51
Monarda 'Kleine Tänzerin' 51
Monarda 'Lilac Girl' 51
Monarda 'Mohawk' 50
Monarda 'Oudolf's Charm' 50, 129
Monarda 'Pawnee' 50, **52**, 103, 129
Monarda 'Perry's White' 51
Monarda 'Pizzicato' 51
Monarda 'Scorpion' 50, 106, **107**, 129
Monarda 'Snow Queen' **49**, 50
Monarda 'Squaw' **24**
Monarda 'Talud' 50, 106, 126
monkshood, see Aconitum
moor grass, see Molinia
mugwort, see Artemisia
mullein, see Verbascum

Nepeta 50, 135
Nepeta clarkei 50, 133
Nepeta govaniana 50, **52**, 94, 98, 103, 123, 129
Nepeta latifolia 50, 134
Nepeta sibirica 50, 133, 134
Nepeta subsessilis 50, 94, 126

old man's beard, see Clematis
Origanum 50, 90, 119, 135
Origanum laevigatum 50, 122, 134
Origanum vulgare 50, 123, 134
Origanum vulgare 'Herrenhausen' 50, **52**
Origanum vulgare 'Rosenkuppel' 50, 126, 129
Oxalis 50
Oxalis acetosella 50, 135

Panicum 81, 122
Panicum virgatum 81, 90, 98, 118, 135
Panicum virgatum 'Cloud Nine' **49**, 81, 110, 119, 129, 134
Panicum virgatum 'Dallas Blues' 81, **82**, 110, 119, 127, 134
Panicum virgatum 'Heavy Metal' **78**, 81, 107, 110
Panicum virgatum 'Rehbraun' **49**, 81, 82, 129
Panicum virgatum 'Shenandoah' 81
pansy, see Viola
Papaver 50
Papaver orientale 35, 50, 135
Papaver orientale 'Beauty of Livermore' 51
Papaver orientale 'Flamingo' 51
Papaver orientale 'Juliane' 51
Papaver orientale 'Karine' 50, 51, **52**
Papaver orientale 'Kleine Tänzerin' 51
Papaver orientale 'Lilac Girl' 51
Papaver orientale 'Perry's White' 51
Papaver orientale 'Pizzicato' 51
Pennisetum 81, 119, 122
Pennisetum alopecuroides 81
Pennisetum alopecuroides 'Cassian' 81
Pennisetum alopecuroides 'Woodside' 81
Pennisetum orientale 81
Pennisetum viridescens 81, **82**, 127
Penstemon 135
Penstemon barbatus 'Praecox Nanus' 51, 123
Penstemon digitalis 'Husker Red' 51
Penstemon hirsutus 51
Perovskia 51
Perovskia abrotanoides 90, 119, 135
Perovskia abrotanoides 'Blue Spire' 51, **52**, 103, 122, 128, 129
Perovskia abrotanoides 'Little Spire' 51, 110, **115**, 127
Persicaria 51, 94, 135
Persicaria amplexicaulis 51, 86, 123, 128, 133, 134
Persicaria amplexicaulis 'Alba' 51
Persicaria amplexicaulis 'Firedance' 51, **52**, **87**, 107, 126
Persicaria amplexicaulis 'Firetail' 51, 129
Persicaria amplexicaulis 'Rosea' 51, **123**, 129
Persicaria bistorta 51
Persicaria bistorta subsp. carnea 51, **52**, 128
Persicaria campanulata 51, 122, 129
Persicaria filiformis, see P. virginiana
Persicaria milletii 51
Persicaria paleaceum, see P. bistorta subsp. carnea
Persicaria polymorpha 51, **52**, **84**, 133, 134
Persicaria virginiana 51, 98, 123, 129
Persicaria virginiana 'Painter's Palette' 51
Petalostemum 51
Petalostemum purpureum 51, **52**
Petrorhagia saxifraga 51, 90, 98, 123, 135
Peucedanum 54
Peucedanum verticillare 54, 94, 98, 119, 133, 134
Phlomis 54, 119, 135

Phlomis macrophylla 54
Phlomis russeliana 54, 110
Phlomis taurica 54, **57**
Phlomis tuberosa 'Amazone' 54, **57**, **102-103**, 127, 129, 134
Phlox 54, **111**
Phlox divaricata 54
Phlox divaricata 'Clouds of Perfume' 54
Phlox divaricata 'May Breeze' 54, **57**
Phlox maculata 54
Phlox maculata 'Delta' 54
Phlox paniculata 54, **57**, **69**, **100**, 103, **107**, 133, 134
Phlox paniculata 'Alba' 54
Phlox paniculata 'Blue Evening' 54
Phlox paniculata 'Düsterlohe' **52**, 54, 106
Phlox paniculata 'Hesperis' 54
Phlox paniculata 'Lavendelwolke' 54, 129
Phlox paniculata 'Lichtspel' 54, **57**, 123, 129, **133**, 134
Phlox paniculata 'Rosa Pastell' 54, 127
Phlox paniculata 'Schneerausch' 54
Phlox paniculata 'Utopia' 54
Pimpinella 54
Pimpinella anisum 11
Pimpinella major var. rosea 54, **57**, 98, 127, 134
pincushion flower, see Scabiosa
pink, see Dianthus
plantain lily, see Hosta
Platycodon 55
Platycodon grandiflorus 55
Platycodon grandiflorus 'Albus' 55
Platycodon grandiflorus 'Perlmutterschale' 55, **57**, 128
plumbago, see Ceratostigma
plumed thistle, see Cirsium
Podophyllum 94
Podophyllum hexandrum 'Majus' 55, **92**
Podophyllum peltatum 55
Polemonium 55
Polemonium carneum 55
Polemonium 'Lambrook Manor' 129
Polemonium 'Lambrook Mauve' 55
Polygonatum 55, 94, 118, 133
Polygonatum xhybridum 'Weihenstephan' 55, **57**, 129
Polygonatum multiflorum 55
Polygonatum verticillatum 55
Polygonum, see Persicaria
poppy, see Papaver
Potentilla 55, 135
Potentilla 'Etna' 55
Potentilla xhopwoodiana 55, 127, 134
Potentilla recta var. sulphurea 55
Potentilla thurberi 55, **60**, 127
Potentilla 'Volcan' 55, 106, 134
prairie dock, see Silphium
prairie malva, see Sidalcea
Primula 46
Primula vialii 51
Pulmonaria 55, **60**, 94, 134, 135
Pulmonaria 'Blaues Meer' 58
Pulmonaria 'Blue Ensign' 58
Pulmonaria 'Cambridge Blue' 58
Pulmonaria 'Dora Bielefeld' 58

Pulmonaria longifolia 55, 129
Pulmonaria 'Majesté' 58, 110
Pulmonaria 'Opal' 58
Pulmonaria 'Pink Dawn' 58
Pulmonaria 'Sissinghurst White' 58

quaking grass, see Briza

Ranunculus 58, 135
Ranunculus aconitifolius 58, 67, 94, 98, 129
Ranunculus aconitifolius 'Flore Pleno' 58
Ranunculus gramineus 58, 90, 110, 135
Rodgersia 58, 94, 119, 135
Rodgersia aesculifolia 58
Rodgersia henrici, see R. pinnata 'Superba'
Rodgersia pinnata 58
Rodgersia pinnata 'Die Anmutige' 58, **60**
Rodgersia pinnata 'Die Schöne' 58
Rodgersia pinnata 'Die Stolze' 58
Rodgersia pinnata 'Maurice Mason' 58
Rodgersia pinnata 'Saarbrücken' 58
Rodgersia pinnata 'Superba' 58
Rodgersia podophylla 58
Rodgersia podophylla 'Rotlaub' 58
Rodgersia podophylla 'Smaragd' 58
Rodgersia purdomii 58
Rodgersia sambucifolia 59
Rodgersia sambucifolia 'Kupferschein' 59
Rodgersia sambucifolia 'Rothaut' 59
Rodgersia tabularis, see Astilboides tabularis
Rudbeckia 59, 119
Rudbeckia maxima 59, **104-105**, 110, 122, 129, 133
Rudbeckia occidentalis 59, 129
Rudbeckia purpurea, see Echinacea purpurea
Ruellia 59
Ruellia humilis 59

sage, see Salvia
Salvia 59, 66, 135
Salvia argentea 59, 90, 110, 133, 134
Salvia azurea 59, **60**, 122, 127, 129, 133
Salvia bulleyana 59
Salvia glutinosa 59, **60**, 94, 122, 129
Salvia glutinosa 'Amber' 59
Salvia hians 59, 128
Salvia nemorosa 59, 107, 129, 134
Salvia nemorosa 'Amethyst' 59, **102-103**, 126, 129
Salvia nemorosa 'Blauhügel' 59
Salvia nemorosa 'Dear Anja' 59, 129
Salvia nemorosa 'Evelyn' 59, 127
Salvia nemorosa 'Mainacht' 127
Salvia nemorosa 'Pink Delight' 59, **60**
Salvia nemorosa 'Rhapsody in Blue' 59
Salvia nemorosa 'Schneehügel' 59
Salvia nemorosa 'Serenade' 59, **60**
Salvia nemorosa 'Tänzerin' 59, 106, 128
Salvia officinalis 90
Salvia officinalis 'Berggarten' 59, 110, 135
Salvia pratensis 59, 62, **90**
Salvia pratensis 'Blue Ocean' 62
Salvia pratensis 'Indigo' 62
Salvia pratensis 'Lapis Lazuli' 62

Salvia sclarea 62, 90, 129, 133, 134
Salvia xsylvestris 59
Salvia verticillata 62, 123, 134
Salvia verticillata 'Purple Rain' **60**, 62, 106, 126
Salvia verticillata 'Smouldering Torches' 62
Sanguisorba 62, 94, 134
Sanguisorba armena 62, 110
Sanguisorba canadensis 62, 118, 122, 129, **134**
Sanguisorba menziesii 62, **64**
Sanguisorba officinalis 62, 98
Sanguisorba officinalis 'Arnhem' 62, 126
Sanguisorba officinalis 'Red Thunder' 62, **64**, **120**, 122, **126**, 129, 133
Sanguisorba sitchensis 62
Sanguisorba 'Tanna' 62, 98, 106, 110, 118, 128, 129
Sanguisorba tenuifolia 62, 133
Sanguisorba tenuifolia 'Alba' 62, **99**, 103, 126, 129
Saponaria 62
Saponaria xlempergii 'Max Frei' 62, 135
Satureja grandiflora, see *Calamintha grandiflora*
sawwort, see *Serratula*
Saxifraga 62
Saxifraga cortusifolia 62, 122
Saxifraga cortusifolia 'Rubrifolia' 62
saxifrage, see *Saxifraga*
Scabiosa 62, 67, 90, 134, 135
Scabiosa japonica var. *alpina* 63
Scabiosa lucida 63, 128
Scabiosa ochroleuca 63, 98, 123, 129, 133
Scabiosa ochroleuca var. *webbiana* 63, 103
scabious, see *Scabiosa*
Schizachyrium 81
Schizachyrium scoparium 90, 110, 118
Schizachyrium scoparium 'The Blues' 81
Scutellaria 63
Scutellaria incana 63, **64**, 103, 110, 119, 122, 128, 129, 134, 135
sea holly, see *Eryngium*
sea kale, see *Crambe*
sea oats, see *Chasmantium*
sedge, see *Carex*
Sedum 63, 90, 119, 122, 135
Sedum 'Matrona' 106
Sedum spectabile 63, 134
Sedum spectabile 'Stardust' 63
Sedum telephium 63
Sedum telephium 'Matrona' 63, 129, 134
Sedum telephium subsp. *maximum* 'Atropurpureum' 63, **64**, 128, 129, **135**
Sedum telephium subsp. *maximum* 'Purple Emperor' 63, 127
Sedum telephium subsp. *ruprechtii* 63, 110
Selinum 63
Selinum wallichianum **33**, 63, **64**, 123, 126, 129, 134
Serratula 63
Serratula seoanei 63, **64**, 119, 122
Sesleria 81
Sesleria autumnalis 81, **82**
Sesleria nitida 81, **82**, 90, 110, 133, 135
Sidalcea 63, 123, 134

Sidalcea oregana 63
Sidalcea oregana 'Candy Girl' 63
Sidalcea oregana 'Elsie Heugh' 63
Sidalcea oregana 'Little Princess' 63, **64**
Sidalcea oregana 'My Love' 63, 127
Silphium 63, 122, 133, 134
Silphium laciniatum 63, **64**
Silphium perfoliatum 63
Silphium terebinthinaceum 66, 98, 118
silver grass, see *Miscanthus*
slender false brome, see *Brachypodium*
small reed, see *Calamagrostis*
Smilacina 66
Smilacina racemosa 66
Smyrnium perfoliatum 66, 94, **95**, 129, 133, 134
snakeweed, see *Persicaria bistorta*
sneezewort, see *Helenium*
soapwort, see *Saponaria*
Solidago 66, 122, 135
Solidago caesia 66, 129
Solidago 'Goldenmosa' 66, **69**
Solidago rugosa **69**, 133
Solidago rugosa 'Fireworks' 66
x*Solidaster* 66
x*Solidaster luteus* 66, 122
x*Solidaster luteus* 'Lemore' 66, 129
Solomon's seal, see *Polygonatum*
Sorghastrum 81
Sorghastrum nutans 81, **82**, 122, 129
Sorghastrum nutans 'Sioux Blue' 81, 110, **111**, 129
speedwell, see *Veronica*
Spodiopogon 81
Spodiopogon sibiricus 81, 128, 129, 133
Sporobolus 81
Sporobolus heterolepis 81, **82**, 90, 98, 118, 123, 126, 127, 129
spurge, see *Euphorbia*
Stachys 66, 135
Stachys grandiflora 'Superba', see *S. macrantha* 'Robusta'
Stachys macrantha 'Robusta' 66, **102—103**
Stachys officinalis 66, 119, 129
Stachys officinalis 'Alba' 66
Stachys officinalis 'Hummelo' 66, 106, 127
Stachys officinalis 'Rosea' 66, **69**, 126, 127, 129
Stachys officinalis 'Spitzweg' 66
stinging nettle, see *Urtica dioica*
Stipa 81, 90, 119, 135
Stipa barbata 81
Stipa calamagrostis, see *Achnatherum calamagrostis*
Stipa gigantea 81, 98, 129
Stipa pennata subsp. *mediterranea*, see *S. pulcherrima*
Stipa pulcherrima 81, **82**, 110, 129
Stipa turkestanica 81, **112**, 128
Strobilanthes atropurpureus 66, 122, 134, 135
stonecrop, see *Sedum*
Stylophorum 66, 94
Stylophorum diphyllum 66
Stylophorum lasiocarpum 66

Succisa 66
Succisa pratensis 66, **69**, 94, 134
Succisella 67
Succisella inflexa 67, 122, 129, 134
sunflower, see *Helianthus*

Tanacetum 67
Tanacetum corymbosum 67, 90, 128, 129
Tanacetum corymbosum 'Festtafel' 67
Tanacetum macrophyllum 67, 94, 129, 134
tansy, see *Tanacetum*
Teucrium 67
Teucrium hircanicum 67, **73**, 103, 119, 123, 133
Thalictrum 67, 94
Thalictrum aquilegifolium 67, 118, 128, 129, 133, 134
Thalictrum aquilegifolium 'Album' 67
Thalictrum aquilegifolium 'Thundercloud' 67
Thalictrum delavayi 67, **69**, 98, 103, 118, 128, 129, 133, 134
Thalictrum delavayi 'Album' 67, 128
Thalictrum delavayi 'Hewitt's Double' 67
Thalictrum dipterocarpum, see *T. delavayi*
Thalictrum 'Elin' 67, **69**, 98, 110, 134
Thalictrum finetii 67, 98, 128
Thalictrum flavum subsp. *glaucum* 67, 110, 128, 133, 134
Thalictrum lucidum 67, **124**, 126, 134
Thalictrum polygamum 67, **69**, 98, 118, 119, 133, 134
Thalictrum punctatum 67
Thalictrum rochebruneanum 67, 98, 110, 134
Thalictrum speciosissimum, see *T. flavum* subsp. *glaucum*
Tiarella 70
Tiarella cordifolia var. *collina*, see *T. wherryi* hort.
Tiarella polyphylla 70
Tiarella wherryi hort. 70, 129
tick seed, see *Coreopsis*
toad flax, see *Linaria*
toad lily, see *Tricyrtis*
Trachystemon orientalis 70, 129
Tricyrtis 70, 94, 122, 135
Tricyrtis formosana 70, 129
Tricyrtis 'Shimone' 70, **73**
Tricyrtis stolonifera, see *T. formosana*
Trifolium 70
Trifolium pannonicum 70, **73**
Trifolium rubens 70, **73**, 90, 126, 129, 133
Trifolium rubens 'Peach Pink' 70, 127
Tunica saxifraga, see *Petrorhagia saxifraga*

Uniola latifolia, see *Chasmantium latifolium*

valerian, see *Valeriana*
Valeriana 70
Valeriana pyrenaica 70, **73**, 94
Veratrum 70, 135
Veratrum californicum 70, 119
Veratrum nigrum 70, **73**
Verbascum 70
Verbascum lychnitis 70, **73**, 90, 110, 119, 133, 134, 135

Verbena 70, 133, 134
Verbena bonariensis 71, 98, 123, 134
Verbena hastata 71, 118, 119, 126, 134
Verbena hastata 'Alba' 71
Verbena hastata 'Rosea' 71, 106
Verbena patagonica, see *V. bonariensis*
Verbesina 71
Verbesina alternifolia 71, 122, **123**, 128, 133, 134
Vernonia 71
Vernonia crinita 71, 119, 122, 129, 134
Vernonia crinita 'Mammuth' 71, **123**
Veronica 71, 135
Veronica gentianoides 'Pallida' 71
Veronica longifolia 71, 94, 119
Veronica longifolia 'Anna' 71
Veronica longifolia 'Lila Karina' 71
Veronica spicata 71
Veronica spicata 'Erika' 71
Veronica spicata 'Rotfuchs' 71
Veronica spicata 'Spitzentraum' 71, 110
Veronicastrum 71
Veronicastrum 'Inspiration' 71
Veronicastrum 'Temptation' 71, **115**, 129
Veronicastrum virginicum 71, 94, 119, 133, 134, 135
Veronicastrum virginicum 'Adoration' 71
Veronicastrum virginicum 'Diana' 71
Veronicastrum virginicum 'Fascination' 71, 129
Veronicastrum virginicum 'Lavendelturm' **24**, 71
Veronicastrum virginicum 'Roseum' **57**, 71, **75**, 107, 129
vervain, see *Verbena*
Viburnum nudum **123**
Viola 71
Viola cornuta 71, 123, 129, 134
Viola cornuta 'Alba' 71, 134
Viola elatior 71, **75**, 128
Viola labradorica 71, 129
Viola sororia 71, **134**
Viola sororia 'Albiflora' 74
Viola sororia 'Freckles' 74, **75**
violet, see *Viola*
viper's bugloss, see *Echium*

wild ginger, see *Asarum*
wild petunia, see *Ruellia*
willow gentian, see *Gentiana asclepiadea*
willow herb, see *Epilobium*
wood anemone, see *Anemone nemorosa*
wood sorrel, see *Oxalis*
woundwort, see *Stachys*

yarrow, see *Achillea*

Zigadenus 74
Zigadenus elegans subsp. *glaucus* 74, **75**